GAINESVILLE PROPER

A Collection Of Poems, Stories, Photos, and Illustrations Celebrating Gainesville, Florida's Historically Black Communities Before Gentrification

Convened by Terri L. Bailey, MA
Illustrations by Turbado Marabou, MFA

GAINESVILLE PROPER: A Collection Of Poems, Stories, Photos, and Illustrations Celebrating Gainesville, Florida's Historically Black Communities Before Gentrification
Convened by Terri L. Bailey

© 2024 Terri L. Bailey
Illustrations and paintings © Turbado Marabou

Some stories, photos, and images were provided by Gainesville community members, partners, historical organizations, and media. All used with permission from the respective person or entity.

ALL RIGHTS RESERVED. This book contains material protected under International and Federal Copyright Laws and Treaties. Any unauthorized reprint or use of this material is prohibited.

No part of this book may be reproduced or transmitted in any form or by any means, electronic or mechanical, including photocopying, recording, or by any information storage and retrieval system without express written permission from the author/publisher.

ISBN: 979-8-9913711-4-8 (Paperback)
ISBN: 979-8-9913711-5-5 (Ebook)

Dedication

Dedicated to the African American Residents of Crosstown/5th Avenue/Pleasant Street and the other Historically Black Communities in Gainesville, FL.

Past, Present, and Future.

Contents

Introduction 9
    Gentrified 13
Erosion of the Roots: The Impact of Gentrification on Historic Black Neighborhoods 17

CROSS TOWN AKA 5TH AVE/PLEASANT STREET **21**
    On Pleasant Street 24
A Conversation with Civil Rights Activist and My Auntie, Miss Rosa B. Williams 26
    This is for My Auntie Rosa B 31
If The Walls of Old Mt. Carmel Could Talk. An Interview with Pastor Gerard Duncan 33
Remembering Miss Clara's Beauty Salon Connie Rawls 41
The Cosby-Parker Legacy – A Discussion With Dr. Carolyn Edwards 50
    The Pleasant Street Elite 63
Cherishing Crosstown with Tina Certain (also known as Sam) 67
Boderick Johnson: Still Crosstown Strong 69
The Art of Pleasant Street: An Interview with Artist and Storyteller Turbado Marabou 71

PORTERS QUARTERS **84**
Replaced But Not Erased: Fighting The Displacement of Black Residents in Gainesville's Historically Black Neighborhoods 86
    Thank You Sistah Desmon 88
The Things Family Teaches You! Tonia Potter 90
Porters Quarters, A Wonderful Place for Imagination Darryl King 92
Peter King: We Never Knew We Were Poor Because We Were Rich With Community 94
Henry Leath – My Life is a Musical 95
Porters Quarters Hidden Folk Art Treasure: Alyne Harris 99
    For the Love of Mr. Henry 107

SPRINGHILL **109**
    The Rebirth of Gainesville's Cotton Club 113
We Will Never Know Where We've Been Unless We Tell The Story
Professor Emerita Vivian Lee Washington Filer 115

    The Cotton Club, Sarah's, Blue Note 117
    Dancing and Partying 119
    Midnight in the Swamp 121

DUVAL HEIGHTS 123
Yvette Clark: From Crosstown to Duval 124
Sharnda Mosley – The Baby of the Bunch 127
Carlos Nelson – My Childhood Meant Freedom Sharnda and Carlos 129
Patricia J. Powers – A Californian in Duval Heights 131

CARVER GARDENS 135
Robert Jammer: Bikes, Basketball, and Lessons from the Big Boys in Carver Gardens 136

LAKE ROAD 138
Tabitha Williams and The Easter Hairstyle 139
Dominique Pinder – Community Events Remind Me of Home 141
Marriette Ellis – My Family Friendly Neighborhood 142

LINCOLN ESTATES 143
Delvon Filer: Continuing a Family Legacy of Service 145
Mr. Sam B Wesley the Second, of Katie Heights, Chronicles the Power of Owning Businesses in Black Communities 147
Tanisha Byers: Good Old Time in Lincoln Estates 149
From Pistol Alley to Lincoln Estates,
God is in Charge Mary Perry Issacs 151

MULTIPLE NEIGHBORHOODS RESIDENTS 154
Alexandria Gibson: Celebrating a Bahamian Legacy in Historic Black Gainesville 155
CARLA LEWIS: A Powerful Advocate for Gainesville's Black Communities 159
Pastor Ernestine Brockington Butler: A Healer of the Body, Soul, and Community 173
    Alachua County 181
A Call to Action 183

Acknowledgements..185
References 188
Photo Credits..189

GENTRIFICATION IN GAINESVILLE

UNDERSTANDING THE IMPACT

Definition
Gentrification is the process of revitalizing and renovating areas, leading to increased property values and the displacement of longtime, often low-income residents. (Source: Merriam-Webster)

Key Facts
- Nearly 20% of low-income neighborhoods have experienced gentrification since 2000.
- Gentrification led to the displacement of over 110,000 Black and 24,000 Hispanic residents from 2000 to 2013.
- Historic districts in Gainesville have witnessed the demolition of numerous buildings since 1982, impacting the city's architectural heritage.

Impact on Gainesville Residents
- The growth of the University of Florida has led to university developments in historically Black neighborhoods.
- These neighborhoods face rising rents, loss of affordable housing, and community displacement.
- Unfair housing policies contribute to stress, depression, and downward mobility among affected communities.

Strategies to Protect Your Property
- **Update Your Will:** Include clear inheritance instructions.
- **Consult an Attorney:** Ensure legal management of inherited property.
- **Know Your Property Rights:** Understand local zoning laws and incentives.
- **Explore Financing Options:** Investigate financial assistance or relief programs.

Data compiled by Bailey Learning and Arts Collective, University of Florida ALP Intern, Kaylynn Nguyen Fall '22

Introduction

I am Terri L. Bailey, and I love being Black. I love being in community with Black folks. I grew up in Gainesville, FL, and primarily lived Crosstown, on both sides of 6th Street. After I became an adult, we spent quite a few years out east on 18th Terrace in Duval. While life wasn't always easy in these Black neighborhoods, most of my memories are good ones.

I proposed this book as an attempt to preserve the essence of our historically Black neighborhoods through the stories, photos, and memories of those who grew up in Gainesville's various Black communities. I was surprised by the similarity of the stories from the various age groups and neighborhoods. Turbado Marabou, a Florida State PhD candidate working on his art education doctorate, identifies this phenomenon as Black collective memory.

Marabou states, "Collective memory in the Black communal experience refers to the shared knowledge and wisdom embodied in Black individuals and communities. This knowledge, passed down through generations, is deeply rooted in shared cultural spaces, where it grows and transforms. These collective memories are authentically shaped within Black communal settings and often span across different generations, regions, and cultures."

I felt a book sharing the stories of those who came of age in the bosom of Black neighborhoods in my Florida city was a great idea. I was given the charge of gathering and sharing the stories of folks from Gainesville's Black neighborhoods. It is important that people have a chance to pay homage to their lineage and their upbringing.

One of the greatest gifts I received from the Most High was growing up in a Black neighborhood. During my childhood, I was fortunate to experience the African admonishment, "It takes a village to raise a child" firsthand. My grandparents and Auntie lived around the corner. My mother, Bettye Hayes Cook, had lifelong friends and acquaintances on every street. The neighbors watched out for you and made you mad by ratting you out through a phone call about your bad behavior. That could result in two to three spankings for a single offense.

I have wonderful memories of getting squeeze cups and other goodies from the candy lady (The Bass House). I recall Miss Mae, the sweet, motherly neighbor who gave snacks to all the kids from her kitchen and her yard (Miss Mae's plums were always extra sweet)! Her husband, Mr. Ike, was mean as hell and never wanted you to play in his yard or even touch their gate. Mr. Ike got sick and went away for a while. One day, he came home, and even though he always yelled at us, we ran to see him because we missed him a lot. He died on his porch that day, watching us running around.

Calvin and I had a fight, and I hit him with a bat because he tried to tell my brother, Jimmy he didn't have to do what I said because I wasn't his momma. His momma, Ms. Polly, and my momma talked about it, and my aunt paid for Calvin to go to the ER. They made us apologize to each other, and he and I are great friends to this day.

One of my favorite stories is my auntie throwing me a party/cookout for my 10th birthday. All the neighbors chipped in and put stuff on the grill and brought Check sodas, cookies, and chips from the Winn Dixie on 6th Street. Chestnut Funeral Home let us use a tent, and we all slept outside all night while the grown-ups grilled, drank, laughed, and told tall tales. They took turns watching us while sitting on a fallen tree on the path by Ma Dank's bootleg house.

Despite loving the days of my youth, our neighborhoods were not perfect. The influx of crack, the lack of jobs that paid a living wage, domestic violence, and poverty were all prevalent in my community while I was growing up. Crosstown/5th Avenue was considered the ghetto, and the only White folks I remember living over there were Miss Paula and her kids. She was a part of our community, and we didn't treat her any differently.

It is amazing to behold how my once undesirable neighborhood is now a feast for the development gods, leaving elderly owners and long-term residents at risk of extinction. In historically Black communities nationwide, gentrification is threatening the continued existence and culture of African American communities in the United States and abroad. As white areas like The Duck Pond and West End Golf Course feel the effects of this gentrification monster, will someone finally listen to the screams from Gainesville's historic neighborhoods?

The neighborhoods gasp for air as they are choked out by unsightly houses imitating the classic architecture of the well-built houses of days gone by. Even the decaying shells of shotgun houses built almost one hundred years ago used better quality materials than the toilet tissue doll houses that continue to pop up. With more expensive housing comes more expensive food prices, taxes, and a lot of businesses the original residents have no use for, which further isolates those who historically occupied these 5th Ave/Crosstown/Pleasant Street/Porter's Quarters/Spring & Sugar Hill streets.

I miss the sounds of children playing in the streets of Crosstown and the smells of dinners cooking as parents call children in from the outdoors. I miss seeing people sitting on their porches in the evening during the summer and spring. Don't think that memory is an antiquated dream of days gone by It is not! The few families that still live in our neighborhoods still do just that. Seeing the elders sitting on the porch or in their yard with a fan and a glass of ice water makes me happy and gives a sweet reminder of a place that used to be home.

Heritage Interrupted: A True Story of Gentrification and a Legacy Lost Porters Quarters Gainesville, FL by Turbado Marabou

Gentrified

This morning before my feet touched the ground
I said thank you Most High for this day most profound
Then I went to my window and looked all around
And my heart grew really heavy, and I felt really down
Because a single black face could hardly be found

Through my old ass windowpane
I looked for the few black folks that remain
Not seeing them here is just so insane
I cried out OH MY GOD Pleasant Street ain't the same

And it just ain't pleasant no more
I feel erased from my own damn story
Because Black ownership y'all haters abhor
And here white occupation replaces Black glory

Tearing down trees where brown babies used to climb
And where black mommas grab thick switches
to beat bad Black behinds
And crying babies ran screaming into jiggling loving arms
Saying come here sugar she ain't mean you no harm
Come on and sit up under this here tree
And get these thousand kisses from yo old Granny

I miss the sound of black children playing on 4th street

Back in the day folks shared the wild-growing loot
And kids and elders picked low hanging fruit
Without fears that angry white men may shoot
And chase you down with Gestapo boots

Worn by a mean white cop
And his pasty-faced wife
Yelling you betta stop
And making you feel scared for your life

Reminding you just because folks move in our hood
Don't mean they like us or mean us no good
The overripe fruit hanging over the fence
Is theirs and not ours and picking it's a damn offense

Yep, that white cop who lives over there
Him and his gnarly ass spouse
Ain't trying to fit in and don't really care
About becoming a neighborhood house

They rather let that fruit rot
And just dissolve into the ground
Than to share their delicious crop
And spread food love around

Nope it ain't very pleasant on Pleasant Street
We feeling isolated and definitely beat
We feeling separated by class and by race
Run out on a rail by those who hate a black face

Who don't seem to value
Having Black folks stick around
Yep I feel all brand new
On my old side of town

Politicians keep on trading
Children's health for federal funds
Three Sistahs on the school board
Disarming racist guns
But unfortunately, change ain't
come

Before Mr. Lovette died

While officials trying to decide
If speaking up will ruin careers
Well, the agendas y'all try to hide
Keep manifesting as citizens' fears

Thank God for them organizers
Fighting for our right to stay at home
Opposing the clueless despisers
Who disregard our right to own

A plot of land or a house
On our historic street
Or a Black spot where we can hang out
Or grab a quick bite to eat

The GAED led by Desmon and crew
Are demanding that black folks get their due
And battling black elders
Who sold out me and you

Why Auntie? Why did you do that????

Seeing Black Lives Matter proclaimed
By signs lining yard after gentrified yard
When their presence means few black lives remain
I know hearing that shit kinda hard

Know we appreciate the sentiment
For we know you've grown to really love this land
While your support is based on good intent
I don't think you truly understand

What it feels like when your white neighbor is uneasy
When you gather with your Black family
Or call police on Black worshipers on Sunday
While they praying for some peace

Cuz their praises woke that napping white baby up

When Moratoriums were pushed aside
When Commissioner Johnson made a plea
To slow it down and take some pride
In our historic communities

Folks like Faye Williams be vocal as hell
Fighting dope boys and the police
Standing firm against those trying to dispel
Porter's Quarters value and relevancy

We will never forget how y'all erased
Seminary Lane and Kennedy Homes
Public housing mercilessly replaced
By student high rises and creepy garden gnomes

But soon the world will see
Gentrification ain't just 'bout our grief
When poor white families finally see
And feel affected by the same classist defeat

And the loss of y'all family land
In the name of eminent domain
May cause y'all to finally take a stand
Against a big business family name

You know like Donald Trump or Keith Perry

But for now, Black folks alone feel the pains
For we're the ones taking the biggest hit
As student housing illuminates our shame
And in the Gentrified chair we sit

Erosion of the Roots: The Impact of Gentrification on Historic Black Neighborhoods

Gentrification has had a profound impact on Gainesville's historic Pleasant Street, 5th Avenue, and Porters Quarters neighborhoods, areas rich with African American history and culture. Once, these communities were vibrant, filled with long-standing residents generationally rooted in the land. Community members invested in the success of local businesses because it meant that everything we needed, from the doctor to the funeral home, from the grocery store to the dry cleaners, was located within a few blocks of most houses. Highly educated professionals lived next door to a blue-collar worker and landscaper with no judgment or pretense. We were truly a community that knew and loved our neighbors. With the assault of gentrification in the name of progress, Pleasant Street isn't as neighborly anymore. Traditional residents are now feeling the pressures of rising property values, increasing rents, and new development projects aimed at attracting wealthier newcomers. This shift threatens to displace elderly homeowners and multi-generational families who have lived there for decades, risking the erasure of the unique cultural identity that has defined Black neighborhoods like Pleasant Street and 5th Avenue for over a century. Many residents struggle to keep up with the rising costs associated with gentrification, as well as the influx of businesses and amenities that cater to new residents but feel out of place for the long-time locals. Gentrification has created a culture of fear and a feeling of erasure for the traditional residents.

In response to these pressures, Gainesville has initiated efforts to preserve and honor the history of the Pleasant Street and 5th Avenue neighborhoods through the creation of a heritage trail. The Gainesville Community Redevelopment Agency has hired the Community Planning Collaborative to complete the project. This trail is envisioned as a way to celebrate and educate others about the area's African American heritage, highlighting significant landmarks, former businesses, and community gathering spots that tell the story of its past. By creating a formalized heritage trail, community leaders hope to raise awareness about the neighborhood's historical significance while also fostering a sense of pride among residents and potentially curbing some of the effects of gentrification. The trail serves as a reminder of the community's resilience and a call to protect its cultural legacy amid ongoing changes. This project has been discussed for decades, and I can't help but wonder if it's being prioritized because of the gentrification of the area. With the diminished number of Black bodies left in Pleasant Street, I see the trail as a memorial of the neighborhood rather than a celebration.

It is important to note that the Community Redevelopment Agency has been working towards "helping" 5th Avenue residents as far back as the 1970s. As I researched for this book, I found an article from 1978 about the City's efforts to bring "redevelopment" to the neighborhood that demonstrated the prophetic fears of 5th Avenue residents about the toll of this redevelopment effort.

TERRI L. BAILEY, MA

Gainesville Sun
Final Edition — 103rd Year—No. 118 Gainesville, Florida, Monday, October 30, 1978 15¢

Redevelopment
City Fights Distrust as It Works to Improve NW 5th Avenue Neighborhood

Related story, picture on Page 5A.

By MARYFRAN JOHNSON
Sun Staff Writer

The old woman rises slowly to her feet at the meeting and asks fearfully, "If I own my home, and I am a taxpayer, then the city cannot take my home away, can it?"

At another meeting, an angry young woman stands and says, "They told me the city was taking my house. Should I move out now? Where I am I supposed to go, anyway?"

These are scenes common to meetings held during the past few months by the city, as word spreads in the neighborhoods about the redevelopment plan Gainesville is undertaking in the NW 5th Avenue neighborhood east of NW 13th Street. Redevelopment will most likely mean tearing down and replacing run-down structures, in contrast to an ongoing housing rehabilitation program which funded repairs of already-existing buildings.

Money from the federal Housing and Urban Development department can be obtained only by submitting a detailed plan on how and where the money will be spent. A long process of neighborhood meetings, advisory committee reports and city plan board approval must be waded through before the city commission can adopt a plan in January and request the $1.3 million in redevelopment money for 1979-80.

The NW 5th Avenue area east of NW 13th Street has been designated as the first priority "target area" for federal money by the city commission. This area encompasses all property between Main Street and NW 13th Street, bounded on the north and south by NW 8th Avenue and NW 3rd Avenue.

Marcia Maleske, a city planner, has worked with the city housing division to draw up a list of 351 properties so hopelessly dilapidated that they are marked for acquisition by the city.

The state Redevelopment Act of 1974, revised in 1977, gives local governments new clout in rehabilitating slum areas. With the power of "eminent domain," the city can condemn property and purchase the land for rebuilding — with or without the owner's approval.

The problem presented by these marked properties is that the owners cannot be notified of the status of their lots until the city commission adopts the whole redevelopment package. So the lists are strictly preliminary, although they spell out which lots should be purchased by the city.

The first area to feel the effects of this purchasing power will be the neighborhood bounded by NW 13th Street and NW 10th Street, between NW 8th and 3rd Avenues — the first phase of the acquisition plan. The second and third phase, moving eastward toward Main Street, won't see any demolition for at least five to seven years.

The city has been holding neighborhood meetings in the NW 5th Avenue area for months now, but talk of actually acquiring property and tearing down buildings is new to the neighborhoods.

"Redevelopment is not the city's decision," Maleske pointed out at one of the meetings. "The people in the neighborhoods said they wanted it. Three years ago, everyone said 'don't tear anything down,' but within the past year, more and more people have called for removal of dilapidated

(More About REBUILD on Page 14)

REBUILD: City Will Help With Rent

houses and bad spots in the community.

"But redevelopment doesn't just tear down houses," the city planner explained. "It reduces the density, creates open spaces, better access to properties and standard size lots for single family homes.

"No one wants to take homes away from people," Maleske said. "But if you decide to go with redevelopment, you've got to accept the fact that something has to go."

Along with the power of eminent domain, however, comes the mandate to provide for the displaced persons. Specifically, the city must offer renters four years of financial assistance with their new rent or a $2,000 loan toward purchase of a home. Homeowners may receive up to $15,000 for their house, plus assistance in locating a new place and $200 in moving expenses.

Officials say they are trying to please as many community members as possible, but decisions from residents are slow in coming.

Joel Buchanan, chairman of the Inner-City Neighborhood Development Association, spoke up at one meeting to warn residents, "If you don't voice your opinions, you'll have no say-so. Now is the time to consider this: it involves you all directly."

Some disturbance has already surfaced at the meetings, especially when people found out that Red's Two Spot and Mom's Kitchen, both businesses in the 1000 block of NW 5th Avenue, were marked for purchase by the city.

"Lula Young (owner of both properties) hasn't been at our meetings so far," Buchanan noted. "But you can bet she'll take an interest now."

Getting people in the area to take an interest in the redevelopment plans has been one of the higher hurdles the city has encountered. "The city can't do it all," Maleske said. "Some of it has to be word of mouth, neighbor to neighbor."

"I encounter a lot of skepticism," Buchanan, himself a resident of the community, said. "These people find it awfully hard to believe the money is free and clear. And when I tell them talking with people, trying to make them understand what redevelopment would mean to them.

"There's a little more concern in the community now, but not really much interest," he admitted. "They're prepared for a change, but they're trying to hold on to all they have — their homes.

"Elderly blacks are very cautious, because so much has been done to them. Once, when white men came around and said, 'here's some money to fix up your house,' they lost their property. They're renters now, and 50 years ago this whole area was black-owned."

Buchanan also expressed concern about people taking advantage of the confusion to turn a fast profit.

"I'm worried about ripoffs," he said flatly. "Like developers coming in and giving someone $5,000 cash for their house, then, boom, tear it down. I counsel waiting."

City officials also are urging people in the community to hold tight to their property until the city commission makes the plan official.

"If you move out before the city makes all this official, there will be no relocation benefits for you," Maleske stressed at an Oct. 9 meeting at Williams' Temple. "Please do not move out of your homes. Wait. We cannot make a move until the city commission approves our plan."

Betsy Jones, the city housing counselor who will handle the bulk of the relocation job, said she believes most of the people will welcome the move.

Jones dealt with the persons displaced by the Seminary Lane apartment project which opens in December in the vicinity of NW 5th Avenue and 12th Street.

"One young couple I worked with didn't realize they could afford a house of their own," she said. "Once the mortgage was arranged and the closing costs were being handled, they used to go every night and sit on the front steps of their new house. They couldn't believe it was all really happening."

"One woman got $2,000 toward a new house," Jones said. "There was drive them around and show them other areas, and they usually warm up to the idea of moving.

"We do run into a little trouble with older people," Jones said. "One person I helped move had lived in the same house for 19 years, but the conditions were unbelievable. The bathroom hadn't been used in years; there were cobwebs all over it.

"Sometimes the only way to make people understand is to say 'I will pay you to move out. I'm here to help. I'm not the bad guy, the one who's throwing you out of your house.'" Jones said.

At a recent meeting, city officials passed around photos of relocated residents in their new homes. The pictures showed neat, modest two-and three-bedroom homes, mostly in the northeast part of the city. Several members of the audience began swapping stories about neighbors of theirs who had moved out and were happy about it.

Mercedes Reese, a citizen attending her first neighborhood meeting, immediately approved. "I know we need betterment," she declared. "I approve of this."

But Etta Turnipseed, a 53-year resident of NW 5th Avenue, didn't like the idea of tearing down parts of her neighborhood.

"This is a good neighborhood," the elderly widow said recently as she sat on her porch watching the activity on 5th Avenue. "There's nothing disrespectful going on here — no raping, or stealing or killing. I never had my house broken into. That's just nonsense that people believes."

Mrs. Turnipseed is a homeowner, which puts her in the minority in the community. Seventy percent of the homes there are rental.

"Now the renters are some folks I don't have nothing to do about," she confided. "I know some of them face to face, but they come and go so quick."

Josephine Veal, another long-time resident of the neighborhood, also likes the area the way it is. "I like to be able to go to down to Red's (Two Spot) and get something to eat," she said, "and there's mighty good

"I guess there could be some improvement around here," Mrs. Veal said. "But I'd like folks to stay and keep their own homes."

Of the 70 percent rental homes in the NW 5th Avenue neighborhood, about 42 percent of the dwellings fall into the "demolition" category, whereas only 20 percent of the owner-occupied homes are in such poor shape. Such housing statistics clearly point out the desirability of more single family homes owned by those living in them," Maleske said. "But we know that most of these people could never afford to own a home," she added.

At least one-fourth of the structures in the entire target area are demolition candidates, according to city figures, and about one-third of the buildings could qualify for redevelopment under federal housing standards.

In the first phase of the redevelopment plan, between NW 13th and 10th Streets, the city plans to buy 22 units and eventually rebuild about 10 of them.

"Some of the lots, which are substandard size now, will be enlarged and include new access to the property," Maleske explained. In the entire area, about 350 properties are marked for purchase, to be replaced with about 300 structures.

City workers repeatedly stress that the acquisition list is tentative and subject to change at almost any stage.

"We're in a difficult position," Maleske pointed out. "We can't say 'hey, the city wants to buy your house to anyone — yet here are lists of properties marked 'acquire.' A lot of people are going to be upset."

These are the properties that have been tentatively marked for acquisition by the city by 1980-81:

- On NW 5th Avenue: street numbers 1001 through 1011; also the corner lot on NW 10th Street. This includes both Red's Two Spot and Mom's Kitchen.
- On NW 6th Place: numbers 1015, 1110, 1112, 1116/1120, 1122, and 1240.
- On NW 7th Avenue: number 1003 and the corner lot on 12th Street.

CROSS TOWN AKA 5TH AVE/ PLEASANT STREET

Photo Credit: Terri L. Bailey

According to the Explore Historic Alachua County website, "The Pleasant Street Historic District in Gainesville, Florida, was established shortly after the Civil War in 1865. A group of African Americans from Camden, South Carolina, settled in the area between Main Street and Grove Street, and Boundary Street, and Union Street. The district was founded as a transition for Black people in Alachua County from slave laborers to freedmen seeking economic independence and cultural self-determination. The district was designated a U.S. historic district on April 20, 1989, and listed on the National Register of Historic Places in 1991."

Known for its educational excellence, Pleasant Street was home to The Union Academy, Lincoln High School, and A. Quinn Jones School, which were all celebrated among Florida's finest academic institutions. Longtime educator Dr. A. Quinn Jones remains recognized as one of Florida's premiere educators. According to Dr. Diedra Houchen,

The historical significance of Professor A. Quinn Jones to Florida, the Gainesville community and specifically the Pleasant Street community where he raised his family should not be underemphasized in scholarship and our shared cultural history. A. Quinn Jones was one of the first graduates from Florida Agricultural and Mechanical University with a bachelor's degree. That he went on to develop the second high school degree-granting institution for African Americans in this specific community of Gainesville, Florida, is a testament to the value of Black institutions and communities. This great legacy of African American schools serving local students still continues today in warm, welcoming spaces such as Caring and Sharing Learning School.

Pleasant Street was recognized nationwide as a Black business mecca, with a plethora of restaurants, bars, stores, a hotel, and a music hall.

Pleasant Street is Gainesville's oldest, continually-inhabited African American residential area, although gentrification of the neighborhood makes this fact hard to believe.

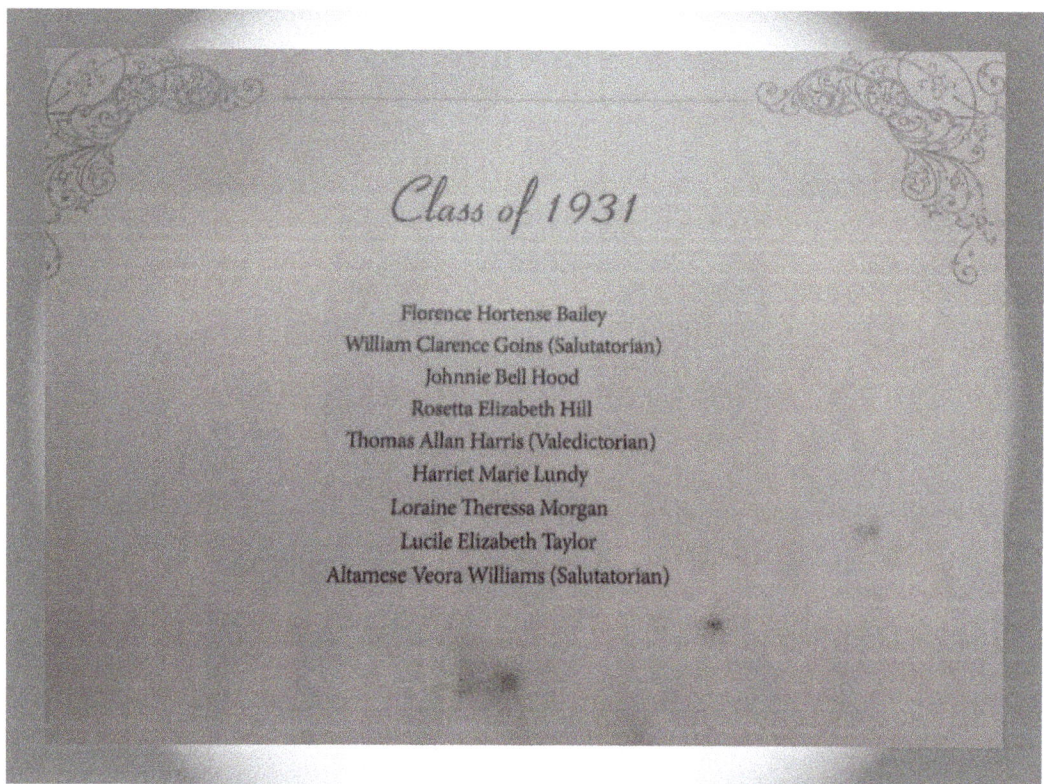

GAINESVILLE PROPER

On Pleasant Street

I arise early awakened by the light and warmth of the sun beaming in my window
The smell of bacon fried hard making my stomach growl and my mouth water
I put on shorts and a t-shirt and run in the kitchen
Trying to sneak a taste of smoking hot black coffee before my Granny playfully pops me
I hang around Grandma Cat's neck while she fixes food for me
My leg swinging over her leg talking endlessly
Waiting to dip my toast in coffee sweetened and weakened for my benefit
One thousand kisses for my Granny who smells like lavender and bleach
"Get off me Gal! Go play!"
Kissing my forehead as she playfully swats my behind and pushes me out the screen door

Onto Pleasant Street

And blue skies, sunshine and fruit and berry trees that provide kids on bikes and those pushing dolls in strollers with sweet, juicy, healthy snacks
Thirsty kids wait for a turn at cool drinks from the water hose
You run, yell, and sweat, and laugh and fight in the dirt until Mommas and Grannies call you inside for love, lunch, and an afternoon nap
So they can watch The Edge of Night turn into Another World quietly, uninterrupted, intently
Miraculously when the TV drama ends, our eyes pop open and we can smell dinner cooking and hear kids screaming our name to come back out and play
You grab a cookie and a kiss as you run out, slamming the screen door behind you
Jumping into games of jacks, hopscotch, and that's my car
When you can play no more you lay on the porch looking up at the setting sun
Dreaming of dinner and tomorrow's adventure
Streetlights indicate the end of child's play and the beginning of adult play dates

On Pleasant Street

While children come into bathe and put on night clothes
Adults play dress up and run outside to friends screaming "Come on Chile let's go!"
Slamming screen doors as they go out to laugh and dance and sweat and curse and kiss
Fried fish sandwiches and cold bottles of beer sometimes lead to side eyes rolling and grown folks rolling in the dirt fighting and messing up their good clothes
Because lies were told as dramas unfold better than those that Mommas and Grannies watch while bad kids take afternoon naps
As I doze off, I hear the sounds of grown folks play dates and think
When I grow up
I'm gonna play outside after the streetlights come on
I wonder how long the streetlights stay on…

Sistahs Heading Out by Turbado Marabou

A Conversation with Civil Rights Activist and My Auntie, Miss Rosa B. Williams

Terri: Auntie, What's your oldest childhood memory? Something that you still remember from when you were little.

Rosa: When I was coming up, we would be playing with the kids next door. We had a White family that lived about a block and a half from us, and they used to come down there and play with us. They would bring food down there for us to eat.

It just looked like then it was more of a community of people supporting each other. We had different things that we would be doing and games we made up on our own. And it was just a bunch of us down there, where Mt. Herman Baptist Church is. Well, right down there in that area, by the laundry mat. See all of that was Black. Where Publix store is now, all that was Black. So it was just a bunch of kids, and we just made programs and things for us to do. . We had more fun than they have now. You know we always stuck together as a group of kids.

Terri: I want you to share something. Now, I ain't trying to embarrass you, but I remember an interesting story about some trouble, you becoming a nanny, and Granny not letting you in one night.

Rosa: You mean, how did I move out? Because she would not open the door. I had a certain time to be home. and I think that I was about 18 years old, and she had told me about being home on time). And I decided I wasn't gonna be home by no 10:30 or 11. So when I went home one night when I wanted to, Momma had the door locked, and a little suitcase with some clothes of mine was sitting on the front porch. And I went around to White and Jones Funeral Home, you know Dorsey 'cause we had been partying, and I told them about how momma had just locked me out, and I stayed there about two nights. And Momma thought I was going to come back, but I didn't. And then they got me a room. Yeah right over in this house here. (points across the street to a green house) that one there. That front room was my room. When Momma put me out, that's the first place I stayed at.

Terri: Okay. At one point, you ended up moving to Tennessee, right?

Rosa: No, I went up there with a White family to work.

Terri: Tell me what you remember about clubbing and going out with your friends and stuff back in the day.

Rosa: I remember the fun what we used to have. Everybody was together. Wasn't no fighting or nothing like that. We all was on the same page and we had fun. Bruh Daniels had his place up there where Santa Fe Community College is, facing 6th Street. Sara McKnight had a place down on 5th Avenue and Fletcher's had his place. And YT had his barbeque place almost up to 13th Street. YT was further down past 12th Street. But that was what we did. Go round to all those places. It was about 15 of us, and we just stayed together and went around to all them places. People from the neighborhood. Some from Porters. And one was from East Gainesville. But most was people from over here in this neighborhood. Now, The Cotton Club was a large place where you could go and dance at and everything. So, we did that. We did a lot of parties there. Sometimes they would have a large band but most of the time they would play music. You could go and dance there and meet your friends. You could not take whiskey on the inside or beer. But somehow or another someone would keep something in the trunk of their cars. But we would go over there to Sarah McKnight's because they closed up at one. She had this, what you call it? A jukebox. And Fletcher's only had a jukebox. At Mamma Lowes, one side of that place was a big eating place, and she had live music in there. Back in those days I used to dance a lot. Everybody danced back in those days. If you didn't dance, they would ask you, "Well, what are you doing here?"

Terri: Well Auntie, anything else you want to tell us about?

Rosa: You know people were more together back in those days. Say for instance if the family didn't have any money, everybody would chip together so they could get the same thing we all were getting. Everybody stayed together. If anything happened to one of them families, everybody was right there, helping out with their family, taking food. It was just more together, and we had fun in those days. Because it wasn't all of them guns and fighting and carrying on. Everyone just really got along. I can't think of not one time we would get into a fight. Now they may disagree. And someone would say, "okay y'all stop this."

GAINESVILLE PROPER

My Auntie Rosa B Williams and My Momma Bettye Cook

This is for My Auntie Rosa B

This is for Auntie Rosa B
Ms. Williams is what she goes by
She short in statue and soft with words
But her power no one can deny

You see when my grandma died
My Momma was just more than a child
My Auntie stepped in to fill granny's shoes
And gave my Mom some time to run wild

I thought Rosa's so cool,
And she has so many friends
We always got to do new doing things
So, I thought she had a lot of money to spend

Now Rosa's no joke, her word is bond
She's too busy to play around
She's busy as ever changing the world
But if you need her she'll make sure she's found

My Auntie is the first person I knew
That ever published a book
Cooking with Rosa at Bell Nursery
Gave parents healthy meals to cook

Did you know that Ms. Rosa
Helped integrate Woolworth's back in the day
When I was chomping on burgers at the counter
I didn't know the price she had to pay

And the parties she gave after the Orange and Blue games
The important folks that came you know well
Thank God most of those shanties are gone by now
Cause those walls had some stories to tell

I used to be mad, cause she was always working
And feeding rich folks black and white
I didn't know at the time they were scarfing down food

She was filling them with ideas on what's right

I would argue with her over the need
To associate with those conservative jerks
But she smiled real nice and said kind words
Making them approve liberal programs that work

I used to swear to heaven above,
I would never be like Rosa B
She works too hard for too little cash
And leads an unnecessary life of poverty

The laugh is on me, cause guess what y'all
I'm more and more like her each day
I love my hood, my race and to share
And the career I picked doesn't pay

My Auntie is awesome and there aren't enough words
To say what she means to me
You all are lucky she loves us so
And I'm blessed to say she's my family

If The Walls of Old Mt. Carmel Could Talk.
An Interview with Pastor Gerard Duncan

Pastor Duncan is one of four Pastors who have occupied the historically recognized church located in Pleasant Street. He is currently renovating the building and preparing to open a community gathering space, which will celebrate the historical significance of the building and help continue the activist future of Gainesville.

Celebrating Old Mt. Carmel
An Interview with Prayers by Faith Paster Gerard Duncan

Terri Bailey: Talk a little bit about your being a part of the original churches in the Pleasant Street neighborhood and being only the third pastor to lead this church out of this building. For this interview, we are sitting in Old Mount Carmel, which is currently Prayers By Faith. Tell us about being in this historic building and how long the church has been established.

Pastor Duncan: I feel grateful. I feel honored in so many ways. It's a privilege to take on such a great legacy. It was actually passed on to me from Reverend Wright and Reverend Mayberry.
They saw valuable characteristics of myself that reflected similarities in them. And so that led to me taking over the responsibility of this building and being entrusted with the future of a story that I believe, at the time, roughly around 2010 or 2012, had stagnated because there had been a change of guard.

For me, being here in this building speaks volumes to the history of not only what took place in the (civil rights) movement of the organization and the first branch of the NAACP (in Alachua County) but also so many valuable meetings that took place for social justice, civil rights - from sit-ins to marches, the whole advocacy as it relates to ensuring that all people, specifically African-American and women, had equal access to a quality of life. So, taking on this work, and not being from Gainesville, and not even being a part of the denomination of Baptist leaders that preached here, and taught here in the congregation, well, for me, was very, very enlightening. I never knew that this building holds so much history. The work that I have here was more about preservation than it was (about) preaching.

I wasn't called to take over this building because I was a good preacher. I was called because of my youthful congregation, and the community advocacy work I was doing was a good fit for the building and to have someone who would continue that great work. I was told by Reverend Wright and Reverend Mayberry that they wanted preservation. They wanted the history of all that took place in Gainesville, in this community, in this building, to be something that was preserved.

And they often told me, "Don't touch the building. Don't change nothing in the building because that's a part of history."

When people come here, there's a value to this building, the architecture, the structure. You know if these walls can talk. If these floors can talk. If these columns can talk, all of the conversations and the meetings and things that took place that ensured the right to equality of life, specifically for the African-American community and women's rights as well (what a great story would be told).

Selected images of the Lincoln High School protest in Gainesville, Florida, Florida Photograph Collection, George A. Smathers Libraries, University of Florida. https://ufdc.ufl.edu/uf00094637/00001

Angered supporters of Lincoln High march in protest of the decision to close Gainesville's historically black high school in mid-year, depriving that year's senior class of graduating together. [UF News and Public Affairs] *The Gainesville Sun*

Terri: What are some of the challenges you're facing now that our neighborhood is experiencing gentrification on such a huge and aggressive level?

Pastor Duncan: I've been in this building roughly since about 2012. What I've experienced, which was very difficult for me to really comprehend or to process, was that the time that I came into the building, the congregation of young people, which primarily was from the age of 23 to 40, they were not knowledgeable of the history. And many of them, who were Gainesville or Alachua County natives, were not aware of what took place in this building.

To me, that was a little bit alarming. They didn't know. And there were conversations, from the inception of coming over to the building, that the building was too old. It wasn't significant to the times that we were in, specifically having a young congregation. And so being a leader of a congregation of young people that did not know that history (made them) hesitant to come over. I got an old soul, so I could see it. And I wasn't willing to compromise what I believe was the restoration not only of a heritage and of a people but of a community.

It was also to bridge that gap and ensure that none of history will be forgotten, specifically among the young congregation. That was very challenging for me…I didn't get a lot of support from my congregation because they didn't see the value and the significance of a building this old. I thought it was beautiful. I thought it was significant because I spent about ten years in Savannah. So, I was around old buildings.

You know, when I was growing up in Miami, I wasn't around old buildings. So, I didn't see it then. But when I moved to Savannah, I saw it. And so that was a challenge because I really couldn't get them to see that. I had to utilize a lot of my influence outside of the congregation and get that support from older people.

People like you; Terri and Miss Rosa taught me about the stories. And that encouraged me. I got some good news. Before I was like, I don't want to do this because I don't have the support of my congregation. And then COVID came, and I lost a lot of people because of it, and I kept going on about history, history, history!

Today, I have a lot of older people who were not from this congregation, but they remember (the history) because they came to meetings, and they're like, we are with you.

And so that was a challenge because when I came in here, I also (wondered) historically - why do so many, if not all, African-American churches and places of significance that have historical or social justice value look like this? And why are the communities that were once plagued by crime and drugs now they're valuable and gentrified. I keep getting letters and having people come by and say, you want to sell to me? I even had a developer tell me that the place is not protected and that there are ways around the landmark.

Told me to my face. You know, there's ways around that. So, there is also a struggle with even getting support from the congregations that once worshiped here. I don't get a lot of support at all. It's (this battle of preservation) not for the faint of heart. Because at any time I feel the heaviness of the repairs that have to be done.

Terri: Why did the original owners build another church? Was it because, again, they didn't see the historical value of keeping this building as their own? What is the future of this building?

Pastor Duncan: The future of the building is to create a community space where the history of the community can be recognized and not forgotten. I think the community itself with all of its changes has a foundation that can never be forgotten.

If these walls could speak, they would speak about a story of a people that came in here who were concerned about our future, a future that we live in right now. They never envisioned in 2024, we'd still be challenged with systemic barriers to having the right to equal access to food, to housing, all of the things that in this room, they made picket signs about, they had conversations about what a future would be like. And I imagine that they felt (it was) so close. That they were gaining ground.

My hope is that I can build upon that and create a welcoming space that people can share ideas, build on their hope, and they can work towards a very constructive and inclusive way of being able to be reminded and afforded that very same history that our seniors, who are elders spoke about in this very room.

I'm committed to that. You know, I haven't abandoned this assignment. It's a slow process, and it's challenging. I've been doing this by myself. Even the best of the best has said "I got your back," but they have not been by my side. But I'm committed to it. I'm almost close. I believe that as we continue to build on the momentum that we have, we'll soon see the fruit of our labor.

We're committed, and we're determined, and we're putting our all into it, and we have not forgotten what I've been entrusted with. And again, you know, I would say this in my conclusion. I'm not from Gainesville. I've adopted this history. I've adopted this story. This building belongs to the people. And so, I'm not going to give up. And this will always be a space where people will be welcome.

There are a lot of people who said their parents were married here. Their parents were eulogized here. They came here for vacation Bible school. This is still your church. This is still your building. It belongs to the community. It is a community space, and it will always be. And so, we're working to ensure that. And we're going to do our best to make sure that this building will never be sold. That it will continue to meet its purpose of being a space where people will be able to come and remember the history of those who've come before us and paved the way so that we can have a better quality of life.

Terri: One of the things we've done with this project is to have people call out their lineage. So, say the name of your family, your mother, your father, your grandparents, whomever you choose to call at this time.

Pastor Duncan: Loretta Knowles and Richard Duncan. I am Bahamian, and both my mother and my father are from Andros Island. My father passed away in 2013. My mother passed away on May 2nd of this year. I uphold their behavior values. That's a part of my life that is dear to me.

And my mother-in-law, who raised me dearly, Tish McGlon, an elder in this community, has also passed away. My wife, Jacqueline Armand Duncan, from Fifth Avenue, Pleasant Street community, and my son, Caleb Duncan, and my daughter, Kylie Duncan. I love my family.

They tell me I do too much. Shout out to them, and Prayers By Faith Ministries, and the people who've supported this great work. We're grateful for their support.

Remembering Miss Clara's Beauty Salon
Connie Rawls

My name is Cornelia Rawls, but everybody calls me Connie. That's my nickname. I grew up in Gainesville, FL. I am the daughter of Clara Griffen. She was a hairstylist here in Gainesville and also an entrepreneur. She was a single mother who raised four children – two girls and two boys – Ella Rawls, Ronald Rawls, Charles Griffen, and me. I applaud her for that because we never wanted anything.

All we ever knew was her working. And she always had a way of providing for us. We never went without. We always had what we needed. We were always able to attend school functions and whatever the community provided for us, like piano lessons, singing in the choir, you know, that kind of thing that kids usually do. I'm really thankful for that because it has gotten me to the point that I am today. I'm a hairdresser too, following in her footsteps. Now, that was something that I never really wanted to do. I had jobs before then, but my mother thought that I should come in and join her. And I did and I worked with her for many years. It's just been a blessing to know who she is and what legacy she has left in this city.

I am from the 5th Ave. area. We lived right on the corner of 7th Ave. and 8th Str. That's all I know because I was born and raised there, and many birthday parties, weddings, anniversaries, and celebrations happened there. My mother loved to entertain, and she always would have people coming in and out.

She always worked in our home. I remember her working from the kitchen and then she added on to the house and made her beauty salon. She worked there for many years and guess what my job was? I was a shampoo girl. She started me out very, very early, maybe 10-11 years old, and I stood on a box, and I would shampoo for her. People really enjoyed my shampoos. So that's one of my specialties now. Everybody says I give a good shampoo.

I'm just so thankful for the upbringing that my mother provided for me and my siblings, even when she felt overwhelmed.

I went away to a boarding school, Boylan-Haven, the one in South Carolina. I went there for two years. My mother got on the train with me because I told her I didn't wanna go. After I got there and got acclimated to the atmosphere, everything began to work out really well for me. (By the way, I went to school with Stevie Wonder's first wife, Syreeta.) It was quite an interesting thing. It was co-ed. The girls had their dorm, and the boys had their dorm, but we went to school together. They had activities, but it was more of a cultural kind of thing. I'm still in touch with at least one of my roommates. Sadly, they've torn the school down. They have a marker there on US 1 but it's not the same. The name of the school was the Boylan-Haven Mather Academy.

In our teens, you know we're transforming, and she was so protective of me because she wanted to make sure that I did what I needed to do.

Terri: What was your fondest memory about growing up in a Black community?

The fondest thing is the camaraderie of the community. We had a whole community! We had barber shops, we had the cab stand, we had a funeral home. There was a little grocery store and a drug store. You know, they had everything that you needed. You knew everybody, and everybody knew you. When it was your birthday, the whole community came together, and they celebrated your birthday. When Christmas time came, it was the same thing. People were back and forth. We were all out in the street playing. I have so many fond memories that, ooh, we just don't have enough time to talk about it all.

I got married out of my mother's house. I graduated high school out of my mother's house. You know I worked there. So, growing up for me was freedom to be who I was. My mother let me be a child, and I had all the opportunities to be that child, and I took advantage of them. I wasn't the worst child, probably not the best one either. My mother said she never whipped us, but she did.

On our street, Miss Cunningham had a monkey and the squeeze cup lady, Miss Rena. These kids don't know about squeeze cups. They don't know about that. It was just Kool-Aid, but we enjoyed it. We were in that time, you know, when if you had your nickels and dimes, you could get things. These are the things that children today don't know about experiencing. It was just such a thrill to be able to do that.

It was mandatory that I had lipstick on, and I had to wear earrings, and my hair had to be right. When it came to my clothes Mom kind of let me feel my way with that. My mother was the lady when it came to being right on spot with dressing and making sure everything was everything. Even when she would shop for me, some things that she would buy, I was like, "Oh my God, Momma!" But this is how she wanted me to dress, even as a little girl. My mother was the lady when it came to fashion, and that's who she was. I just loved that about her, and I'm glad she left that with me. Even today, in the salon where I work two days a week, when I finish eating, I put my lipstick on, and the ladies say, "Where is she going?" I'm not going anywhere. So, you know this is what I do.

My mother attracted a lot of people. People liked her personality. She was a regular person. She wasn't standoffish. She welcomed everybody. She liked the people on the street. She liked the higher-ups. She liked them all!

She even had the Ebony Fashion Fair models come to her salon, and she was able to do their hair one year. Yeah, she was the go-to person; if they were selling tickets for this or tickets for that, she was the lady to go to. That was Miss Clara.

Children today are missing the love of the community. The caring and the concern. People loved you. You didn't even have to be family. Everybody was your cousin, or you felt related to them. We were allowed to, you know, play together, and share things together. You know, we shared the sicknesses and the deaths and the good and the bad. All the things that would help you to grow, to mature into the person you need to mature into. I think that for the kids today, there's silence there because of the electronics. As long as you're on your computer or your phone or something and you're not bothering me, that's fine. Parents don't encourage their children to go outside to play or to mix and mingle. They don't even know the children next door - if there are any children next door. I think about how we made our own games, and we played hopscotch and made our own sticks and played baseball. We rode our bicycles, and we did it as a community - not just me and my brother, a community. We all got together and came down to the area where the main train station was and skated. That was a big deal!

The kids are missing a whole lot because I think that their parents didn't get it. It (the sense of community) sort of faded away, so what they don't know, they can't teach their children.

You know, I don't think there are any kids there (in our neighborhood). If they are, we don't see them. I mean, at Christmas, everybody was out on either skates or bicycles or something. You were walking, talking, laughing, and making too much noise and had to move on down the street. It's so sad that even at Halloween, you don't see the kids out. Their parents take them to the mall, and they pick up whatever is there, and then they come back. All of those things really just kind of made the community and kept us solid. They're just not there anymore.

Even the churches were more involved. I grew up in Mount Pleasant, and there was always something to do. It was Larry (Saunders) and I and my two brothers, and we got on 7th Ave and walked down to Mt. Pleasant, whether it was choir rehearsal, Easter practice, Christmas practice, children's day, or whatever. It was something that kept us going and moving in the direction that we needed to move in.

Gentrification is a travesty. It destroyed the community. It destroyed families. It's destroyed businesses. I wonder if I am the only one that feels like this. I went over to my mother's property, which has been sold now, and nature has taken over. It looks horrible! It's the epitome of greed, I think, and these people know this when they do this. Why won't they choose somewhere else? They choose these properties because they know they'll be valuable. They've paid a small amount for the greater amount that they will receive from it. It took me about four years to go back over to my mom's old house because I just could not take it. When I think that gentrification has just destroyed that whole area - that historical area, (well what is supposed to be historical), but they're making it something else. I think now somebody says it's called Renaissance or something. I think that it's just really sad, because if you don't have a focus on what it was, or pictures or anything like that, it's just wiped from memory. But when you can go back and say ooh, Miss so and so used to live here, or they had a little store down there, or, the beauty shop was here, or the school was down there…

I went to A. Quinn Jones, but it was Lincoln High School before it became A. Quinn Jones, and so I didn't get to go to Lincoln. My mother went to Lincoln on 7th Ave. But we had to be bussed over to Lincoln High School. And it's just such a sad, sad situation to see our communities go like that. And they've fixed it where it's impossible for you to live there. They've raised the taxes, and they've got all these stipulations, things that you can't possibly live up to. So, what do you have? You don't have a choice in the matter.

I think that they exaggerated the whole thing (crime and drugs in our neighborhood) to make us look like bad, but we were nothing near that bad. We didn't do anything that anybody else did. Crime is higher now than it was when we were coming up. They used that to get what they wanted to get.

I just don't know who else is going to come behind us. There's nobody else to come behind us because people are selling out or they have sold out. So, you don't have anything to come back to and claim this is this or that was that; it's just gone. It's very hard and I have cried and shed many tears behind it. My mother and my mother's mother's mother lived in that area, so we go way way back. For us, as the people that we are, to just give it up, you know, without a fight, it's just kind of bad.

There's just nothing there (at Miss Clara's house). Most people of our generation, that's all they know is Clara's. Someone took her sign. I don't know who did. They put it on social media with the caption; "what happened to Clara's sign?" Code enforcement had no clue. There's just nothing there. After I'm gone and my brother is gone, there will be nothing. His children just know that Grandmother lived there. They don't know the history.

I am so honored that I'm a part of this piece of history. That's been one of my desires, to always keep my mother's name afloat. So, people don't ever forget who she is or was. Because she was my mother, and she held fast to what she believed. She worked in the community, she served in her church, and she was just all around. I don't want her legacy to die down. I've had some drawbacks with certain things that have tried to tarnish her legacy, but I refuse to let that happen. She retired at 81, and I hope this project will help her legacy go down through the years even after I'm gone.

GAINESVILLE PROPER

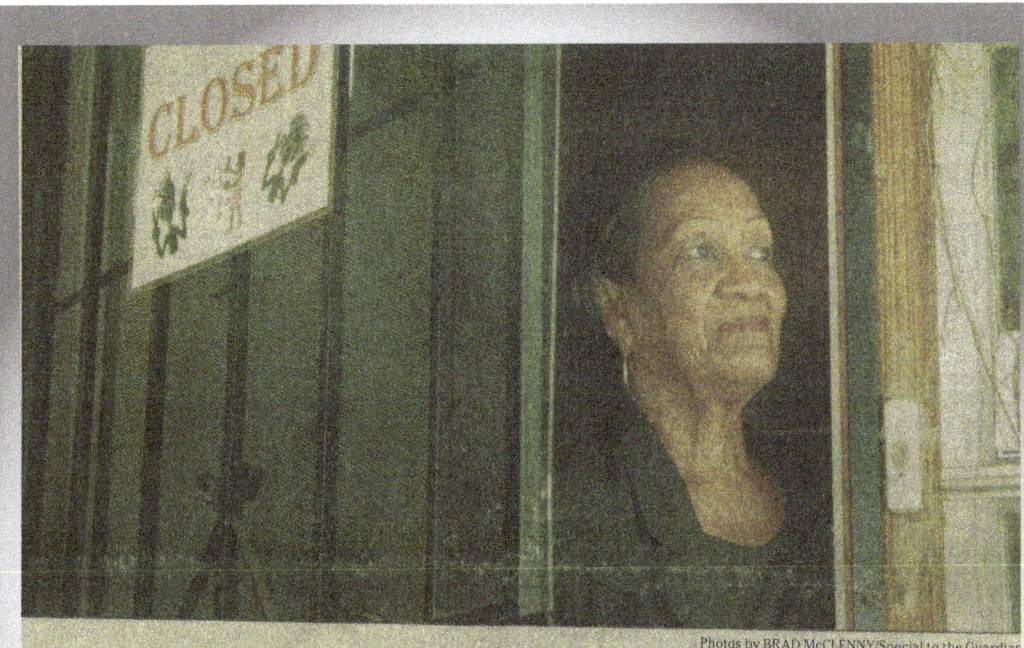

Photos by BRAD McCLENNY/Special to the Guardian

Clara's Beauty Salon closes its doors

By CLEVELAND TINKER
Special to the Guardian

One of the most recognizable businesses in Gainesville's black community has closed its doors for good.

Clara Griffin, the owner of Clara's Beauty Salon in the NW 5th Avenue area, retired in early July.

"After working as a beautician here for more than 50 years, I just decided it was time to retire," said Griffin. The salon, attached to Griffin's home, are located on the corner of NW 8th Street and 7th Avenue.

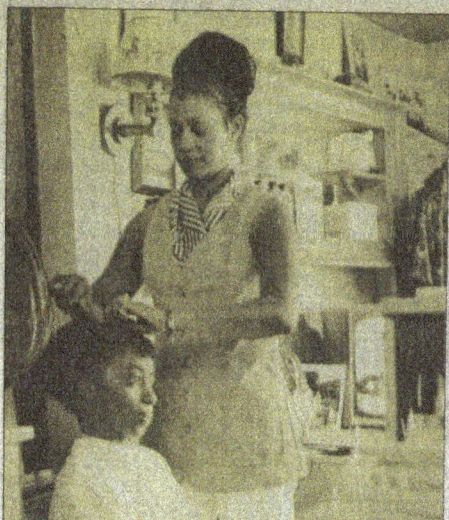

Above: After more than 50 years in business, Clara Griffin has closed her beauty salon in the NW 5th Avenue area. Left: In this photgraph from 1971, Clara Griffin is shown doing hair in her shop.

GAINESVILLE PROPER

The Cosby-Parker Legacy – A Discussion With Dr. Carolyn Edwards

Terri: Tell us about who you are and the neighborhood you grew up in.

Dr. Edwards: Well, I start with two people. One is Eliza Caro, and she is my Great-grandmother, my grandfather's mother. The other is Jumima Whittaker, who is my great, great-grandmother on the other side. My great-grandmother, my grandfather's mother, Eliza Caro, built it, somewhere around 1870. Well, I know my grandfather was born in 1877. Before 1877, she procured a little house that's on the end of this property and started what became our; I call it, our family legacy. She built a house; my grandfather enlarged the house and moved it to 4th Street. It was originally on 3rd Street, and there's a reason behind that, which has to do with the neighborhood. And Jumima Whittaker is my oldest known ancestor, and she was born in 1820. She's listed in the 1870s census as being 50 years old at that time, and she's buried at Mount Pleasant Cemetery.

There's a lot of history that goes into it. And my family legacy, as I call it, dates back to that. And they started it. I mean, they started it with virtually nothing. Eliza Cato was - Cairo, not Cato - my neighbor's was Cato.

Anyway, Eliza you know, started from nothing. She had been an enslaved woman, and she made a way, as they say, out of no way. She worked in people's houses. She did what she could. She sold Avon products, and she was able to, with that, to send my grandfather to college, to Fisk, it was Fisk College, Fisk University, and Meharry Medical School. And he became a doctor, and traveled a bit, but came back to this particular house, well, the one that was here originally, and this was his office. And you know, even when I was growing up before he passed, he lived here, and we had to stay upstairs while he was working, and then he retired. But my mother's family had seven children.

Terri: Why did y'all move from 3rd Street?

Dr. Edwards: My grandfather had seven children - six girls…Before downtown Gainesville proceeded this far from 8th Avenue this way on 3rd. Main Street, 1st, 2nd, 3rd, and 4th Street were black neighborhoods. And so, the neighborhoods, and of course, you're talking about Jim Crow era and segregation - the black neighborhood was here, and it was stationary, and the white neighborhood was moving like this from here to University.

So, the house there, (pointing to the back of the house) even when I was growing up, there was kind of a dividing line. I mean, there's no fence or railroads or anything, but you know, this part of 3rd, 2nd, and 1st Street was all white, and we didn't go in that area. But my grandfather's house was right on this corner. He moved it to 4th Street, which was a black area, because in his words, and this is what he says, "I didn't want those people saying ugly things to my pretty little girls."

And that's why he moved the house, and you know, the yard is still back there, and it was a buffer. I mean, we used to play in the yard and use the yard, but the house faced this way, which is 4th, 5th, and 6th, but 4th Street and, all of this area, has always been or was traditionally all Black. And that's why he did that.

Terri: When you first said that I immediately considered that we knew growing up in the 70s that we did not go on this end of 3rd Street unless we absolutely had a destination. There was no wandering around or walking in that neighborhood.

Dr. Edwards: Yeah, I'm old enough that downtown was downtown, and we walked down that way. But between this 3rd Avenue here and 5th Avenue, we didn't go; we would come around this way and go on 5th Avenue, but not on 3rd Street. …interestingly enough, my grandfather, my great grandfather, lived on 1st Street right behind Main Street, where…it was Black…near Mount Pleasant church… all of that little area in the 1870s, up until recently, was where Black people lived.

I'm talking about the 1870s, and you're talking about the 1970s. And really, the change started to happen probably in the middle of the 70s, and by the 80s, gentrification was in full force. And now it's not complete, but it's getting close to that.

Terri: Your grandfather moved the house to 4th Street. Tell us about that.

Dr. Edwards: Well, he moved the house to 4th Street, and it was just a little shotgun house. But through the years, he added two stories. After his renovation, it was two stories with a front and a back porch. And off the surrounding porch was the entrance to his office. People could come into the front door, but his actual exam room was back off that porch area. So sometimes people would sit outside because there wasn't really a lot of space. There was a little, what would be called a waiting room, which is the front foyer. He had his practice here until he died in 1954.

Terri: Could you say his name again?

Dr. Edwards: It's Julius Parker. Julius Augustus Parker Sr, because he did have a son that he named the same name. They don't talk about it too much, but his father was also Julius A. Parker, but he died very young, Eliza Caro's husband. It was not something that was in the books as her husband, but Julius Parker, the real Julius Parker Sr, was the father of my grandfather.

Terri: And so, your grandfather had a thriving practice.

Dr. Edwards: Yes. A medical practice.

Terri: Was he only servicing Black folks?

Dr. Edwards: For the most part, Interestingly enough, he also had a pharmacy that was off of Main St, near University, and about 1st Street, which served the whole community. As a doctor and a professional person, he was allowed to do certain things.

There were incidents when White doctors couldn't treat people, and he would treat them. When they wouldn't treat White patients, he would, but it wasn't anything that was a regular practice. His regular practice was neighborhood people who were Black people.

He had six children, seven children, and my mother was next to the youngest. His son was the youngest. You know, there was a big joke that he kept having children until he had a son, because he had six girls. One of them, unfortunately, died when she was nine years old. But his five daughters grew up here. They went to school here, starting with the Union Academy, and then Lincoln, which was elementary - no such thing as middle school, but elementary and high school. And they graduated from Lincoln.

Education was critical to my grandfather and to his children, so they all went to college, many went to Fisk because that's where he went, and that's where my mother went. And they all became professionals. The women, primarily teachers, because that's what women could do, and they always said, you know, my mother would have been the best doctor, but that wasn't something that was considered an option, so she became a teacher. She was also a medical lab technician, even though the medical field was not very open to Black women. That's why she went back to school and became a teacher, as did all of my aunts. My uncle, the youngest, was a chemist. He was a researcher at the University of Michigan. And my Aunt Carolyn, the oldest, the one that I was named for, was a physicist. You know they recently named the school for her - Carolyn Parker Elementary.

I'm named Carolyn for her, and the reason was, as in many families, she basically raised my mother. My grandmother had many children, and she worked. She was a teacher. She taught before she was able or allowed to get a degree - if you went to eighth grade, you could be a teacher. Then eventually she, you know, got her degree and was certified and worked at Duval Elementary.

My grandmother had all these children; the oldest ones, as was a tradition, would take care of the youngest ones. My mother being younger, my aunt Carolyn, (being older) took care of her. She was pretty much grown when my mother was born, so she helped put her through college, she helped get clothes and things for her. When my mother had me, her firstborn child, she named me Carolyn. Carolyn was a physicist. She worked on what became the nuclear program, little known to them, it was for the atomic bomb. She went to MIT. She did everything except get her doctorate. She was working on a doctorate when she died at a fairly young age. She had multiple sclerosis and leukemia, which was a result of working with the chemicals.

And my other aunts were math and science teachers, except one who was a librarian. So, to say education was critical to them and - just back to my aunt for one quick second - that's why I was driven to get my doctorate because I had to live up to my aunt's reputation. I had to finish what she wasn't able to finish.

My mother met my father when they were both at Fisk and they got married while they were still in college. He went on to dental school in Missouri, where I was born, to do an internship, and he was an oral surgeon. When they allowed him to, he had hospital operating privileges. But when he didn't, he teamed up with a doctor, CW Cullen Wadsworth Banks, and built a little office on 6th Street, which is the dividing line between Pleasant Street and the 5th Avenue neighborhood. And he did that in the early 50s. He graduated from dental school, did a residency, and was drafted into the Army, and went to Germany as a dentist. So, I did spend a few years in Germany as an Army brat. He came back and started a practice, which he kept going until he died in 2004. And fortunately, they're still using the building. Youth Build, an educational training program, is there. I'm glad to see it being used for positive things.

Terri: So, was he one of the first Black dentists in the area?

Dr. Edwards: It was like one at a time. There was Dr. DeBose and Dr. Stafford. There were about three or four. There have been Black doctors, dentists, and educators in Gainesville almost from the start. So, my great-grandfather was a doctor. I mean, he was trained in traditional medicine, healing.

Terri: When your dad finished in Germany, you all moved back here? Tell me about your upbringing and your life.

Dr. Edwards: Well, I grew up here. I came here when I was one year old after my father finished school. And for two years, we were in Germany, and I was like four or five when I came back here. I went to A. Quinn Jones Elementary School, and the high school moved to what is now Lincoln Middle School. It had changed, it's the same place that had been Lincoln Elementary and High School, the building on 10th and 7th Street and 10th Avenue, that Red Brick building.

I went to first through sixth grade there and went to seventh through ninth at what was called New Lincoln, in the Southeast, the new school that they built, and they changed that to an elementary school. When I sit here on my porch and I look out, it's deserted. We used to play on these streets. We used to go skating. I got marks on my knees. We used to ride our bicycles. We used to have relay races. I used to play marbles, you know, because I liked to do that. And there were children. Miss Oleatha Rutledge, right across the street, she had her grandson next door. The George Family, also next door, had their children further down. Florence Williams, Henley Williams lived there where Mrs. Hindley, who was a noted educator, lived right down the street.

One of the things that I remember about my childhood is that we weren't really reigned in. I mean, we were disciplined. We knew what we could do, and we knew what we couldn't do. But it wasn't like our parents were always looking at us because we had neighbors. I got the nosy neighbor, Miss Cato. You know? And when we got to be teenagers and wanted to go to the recreation center to the little dances they had there, and we girls had our little fellas walk us. They (the boys) couldn't walk past the corner because Miss Cato would be sitting, she used to sit on the porch, then she sat inside and looked out the window. And she would report if I were walking, and I got too close to the railroad tracks. Somebody would call my father and say, "Doc, your daughter's too close to the railroad tracks." But we just basically went outside to play. They didn't have to entertain us. We figured out what to do. And the rule was, when the streetlights come on, you have to be home.

We just would roam around and do whatever, go find frogs and play. I thought I was gonna be a scientist, so I said, I gotta deal with worms, frogs, and stuff. That changed. But the point that I wanted to make is that we had an open life because it was a safe place to be, and people would take care of you. And as children, of course, we got upset.
You know, "Why you gotta do that?" And I couldn't wait to leave because of that. But they were watching out for us and our parents didn't have to have us on a leash.

And they would tell us, you're not supposed to walk down 5th Avenue because it was grown folks stuff there, not because it was dangerous or anything. When we walked to school, we were supposed to walk down 4th Avenue and go around there. Of course, we walked straight down 5th Avenue. And straight back home because we had to stop and get a cherry Coke or something at Cato's Sundry on 5th Avenue. And The Rose Theater was there, just two blocks down from there.

In school, I was in the Lincoln High School band from seventh to ninth grade. I played the clarinet because my father had played the clarinet. And he even thought he was a little musician and went out on tour for a couple of weeks and came back and decided to go to school and be a dentist. I went as far as the second clarinet. And I was the sweetheart of the band one year and had to sit on the little open car and ride in the parade and stuff. And that was a big deal.

Marching with the band was no joke. Because the idea was to go to FAMU and be a part of their band. We would go up and down the street. The band director was Jerry Miller. Interestingly, his wife was also named Gerri Miller. She was over the chorus. After school we would have to march up and down the street in front of Lincoln. And he said, "Get your knees to your nose." And he wasn't playing. We had to get and play music and learn little dance steps. And it was all cool. It was an experience.

In my little prepubescent years, I was a little chubby. But I was slim and trim by the ninth grade. All that marching up and down every day. And then in the summers, there was a pool. And we'd go swimming. I was on the swim team for about two months. I learned swimming from Mr. Mickle. Stephan Mickle, and also his brother Andrew. But mainly Stephan.

Terri: What do you remember about going to dances at the center?

Dr. Edwards: I remember going, and you know, it's where I think they have a police substation in the community center now. I remember, the songs that I liked, I liked the fast songs. When the slow songs came on, I usually tried to go to the bathroom because the wrong person was gonna ask me to dance. But it was just some place to go, something to do. We complained about not having enough to do, and when I look in hindsight, we had a lot to do. But, yeah, it was a place to go on weekends, I think it was Saturday, we didn't stay out too late.

My children were born in 75 and 78, and by then it wasn't an option as a place to go. My grandchildren visited and stayed here over Christmas holidays, and they walked around, and we went down there, and they shot hoops at the basketball courts, and my grandson looked at me and said, "Where are the children?" And you know, this was holiday time, vacation time, and there was nobody. I think one or two people came over to that basketball court.

There are no children here, and just in general, society has changed. The parents, my son, and his wife, drive their children to the park so they can ride their bicycles or play basketball or whatever, because just nationwide, it's like that. You don't see children outside playing.

I remember being little, and they said, "Duval Heights and Lincoln Estates," and I was jealous, I wanted to move over there in one of those new houses they had over there. We had this old house, been here over 100 years, who wants to stay over here? So, I left. My sisters left, except one sister lived here for a good amount of time. We left and went either to other parts of the city that were newer; or left the city and the state altogether.

Terri: Tell me what happened to the family house. This will be the third iteration of your family property.

Dr. Edwards: The original house was the foundation for what was a two-story house, reminiscent of the current house. But that house was destroyed in a fire in 2017. And we were here that December. We were here trying to decide what to do with the house because none of us were living here, but we knew we wanted to keep the house. Then after the first fire, there was a small fire in the attic because somebody threw a firecracker or something up there. And the fire people came, put it out completely out and turned off the electricity.

But at three o'clock in the morning, the house was totally ablaze, and it burned down. It totally burned to the ground. My mother, who was very good with finances, was very good with insurance and all those things. And she had insurance that was sufficient pretty much for us to rebuild the house. We rebuilt it. It's smaller, believe it or not, it looks big, but it's smaller than the house that was here. And it has some features like the porch is the same, but a lot of other things are smaller and more scaled to what we could do with the insurance that we had. And then as things happened, my husband and I decided in our retirement that we would move here. Unfortunately, my husband passed away.

I sold the house that I had in Rochester, New York and moved back here in 2022.

GAINESVILLE PROPER

Parker Cosby House   Before 1877
The birthplace of Dr. Julius W. Parker in 1877, this house was moved on site some time aft[er]
1910 from Arredonda Street to Grove City (now Fourth). Mrs. E. A. Cosby, the youngest

The Ellis House on 5th Avenue: Jimmy and Janice Ellis Recall The Days

Janice: We used to live at 812, which was on the opposite side of the barbershop right here (on 5th Ave), in this building (the old Gainesville Community Redevelopment Agency/CRA), where the parking lot is now. We were living there and then in 67, 68 we moved here.

I'm Janice, Janice Ellis originally, but I'm married, which now makes me Janice Morris.

We had neighbors in the lot over here in these two lots (across the street) that we grew up with and played with. There were neighbors here (across the street) where the garden is that we also grew up with and played with. It was really, really good. It was good for us, now I don't know about our parents because we don't know what they were going through, but for the kids, we had a wonderful time! I enjoyed my childhood. I really did. We went to A. Quinn Jones. I went to Bell Nursery. I went to J.J. Finely, Westwood, Gainesville High School, of course we all graduated from there in 1978.

Terri: Jimmy, tell us about you.

Jimmy: I'm Orian James Ellis, Jr., I grew up at 906 NW 5th Avenue, Gainesville, FL. Crosstown. My mom and dad were Orian Ellis, Sr and Rheatha Mae Ellis. Those were the strongholds. My mom was the matriarch of the neighborhood. She took care of everybody. My older siblings were Sharon Roundtree, Pamela Copeland now, but was Ellis. Gwen Ellis, Janice Ellis, Carmen Ellis, and my brother Wayne. I was the younger of the seven.

One thing that stands out to me as a memory, especially with you Terri, was them turning on the water from the fire hydrant. They would turn on the fire hydrants for us and man it'd be like we were at the beach almost, because that was kinda all we had at those times. But that was a lot of fun too and our childhood was awesome. There were a lot of us, and the older people kept us in line. We had parents all the way up and down the road and up and down by the neighborhood. We weren't running around doing stuff we had no business doing; we were just being kids having fun, exploring, creating new games, and playing old school games. Just being a kid and having fun. We've done some creative stuff around here, man I ain't lying we did.

People don't believe that we built our own underground tunnels and stuff. Man, we were creative. We had time to do it because we weren't sitting in the house - you know let's just say every generation is different - these kids sit in the house, play with gadgets, and do all this stuff. We were outside and when you're outside you are out there where stuff is living, and we were living! Yeah, so that's the way I look at it, man. I feel like I'm so blessed to have had the opportunity to grow up around people like me. And we got along. There was no fighting, biting, well as kids, you have some of that, but as a community, like I said, the whole community took care of you.

When you got out of line one of the older boys in the neighborhood would tell you, "Hey boy! What came out of your mouth?" and they'll straighten you out! And the women as well. I don't mean the grown women. I'm talking about the ones that were a little bit older than you. Respect was everywhere. That's something that's missing. Respect and discipline. You say something to some of these kids now, some of these young men, man you gotta really be careful how you approach them, because they'll fly off the roof! So nowadays you kind of have to be a little more scared about it.

I remember back in the day, dribbling the ball out here and guys telling me, "boy you're gonna be good at this one day." Then another guy said, "No, you're doing it wrong." He would take the ball and say, "Now get it back!" And you had to get your ball back if you wanted it. You got the love, but you also got the toughness.

Terri: Tell me about your history with the Rosa B Williams Center.

Jimmy: I was the community director at the Rosa B. Williams Center for six years, and I would honestly say most of these, I'm gonna call them my children, still come by my house today to see me and to thank me for helping them develop into who and what they've become. These kids are doing well. Those were some of the greatest times of my life. To be able to visualize it and see it happening before my eyes. I was just doing my job, but the way they tell me I touched them is amazing! I do plan on having a reunion with my children and I would love to use the Rosa Williams Center.

Terri: Gainesville has, in terms of preserving and loving the Black neighborhoods, loving neighborhoods in general, has really dropped the ball.

Jimmy: Well, I mean, just consider the fact the amenities that we have on the east side of town compared to the amenities are on the west side of town where you got all the hospitals, all the grocery stores. I mean what are our people supposed to do for these things? I mean, come on, guys! Yet you keep pumping money out west, now for some Olympic thing and can't build a hospital or something decent over here for Black people. It's an old community over here (Crosstown). They should be treated with some respect and that this city doesn't … They've never done that, so I'm not surprised. Again, this community sustained itself back in the day. There wasn't nothing coming from the outside.

My uncle was one of the farmers that came by here and gave and sold stuff to people. People sold everything, ice, fruit, vegetables, fish. Everything you needed!

Janice: I mean everything!

Jimmy: Yep, everything you needed right in this community! You had the funeral home, the doctor, many churches, and for entertainment, bars, and restaurants.

The Pleasant Street Elite

This is a Pleasant Street shoutout y'all
And I'm here to run it down
Let me inform you if you don't know
The importance of growing up Crosstown

Back in the day when my moms was young
And running with her crew
This was the Black business Mecca
With food and music and plenty to do

Now we all know
That you were never EVER supposed to go across 6th St
But they were bad kids, so they looked both ways
And slyly began to creep

There were Cato burgers, pork chops from Mom's
And a sausage sandwich from Mr. Fred's grill
And when they all grew up and could stay out past dark
They ran the streets seeking fun and big thrills

They'd stop at Red's 2 Spot,
Mr. Woody's shop,
The Beer Tavern and the Wigwam Lounge
During the holidays you'll find everyone at Fletcher's
Chillin' while they're back in town

I cannot forget lying in my bed
Listening to the grown folks shine and trip
I learned way too much about their business
From the sounds of the Sunset Strip

As for me and mine I have to recall
When they turned 5th Ave into a waterfall
Memba getting beatings from all the moms
One hard smack from each
They ain't mean you no harm

You bet not do nothin'
You bet not mess up
I bet Duncan Brothers
Will come get yo butt

Oh, you still talking
Thought I told you to shut up
Just say one more word
And I'm calling Chestnuts

Don't get me wrong we did more than party
Pleasant St's rich in history
Look up Union St. School, Lincoln, and A. Quinn
To see how we rolled academically

We had Dr. Cosby and Dr. Banks
Practicing medicine up the block
Mr. Oscar Gilbert repaired our shoes
And Ms. Sanders kept our clothes looking hot

In Pleasant Street God reigns supreme
We're a spiritually gated community
Mt. Pleasant, Mt. Carmel, Greater Bethel, and Friendship
Gave the word to those willing to receive

I could go on, but I'll stop now
And let your memories take flight
I'll close with this
Till the day I die
I'll thank God I'm a Pleasantite!

GAINESVILLE PROPER

Duncan Brothers Funeral Home

Chestnut Funeral Home

The first Mt. Carmel Baptist Church was founded in 1893 at 601 E. Grove Street. This building served the congregation until the new brick church was consecrated in 1946.

Cherishing Crosstown with Tina Certain (also known as Sam)

Terri: Greetings! Please say your name, your lineage, and the neighborhood you're representing.

Tina: My name is Tina Wilson Certain. I am also known as Sam, and I represent Crosstown. I am an elected official of the Alachua County School Board now, but I worked professionally as an accountant.

I am the daughter of Joanne Wilson, who was raised by my maternal grandmother, Clara Wilson, also known as Mama Tina of The Alley.

Terri: Tell me about a cherished childhood memory growing up in Crosstown.

Tina: There are so many, but if I had to pick one, I would have to say it is playing on the lane. The lane was 6th place, 6th Avenue, 5th Avenue. Then going into Mom's Kitchen for lemonade or fruit punch. Being told by Miss Lula and Mr. Frank to "go wash up." And when we would fold boxes for them, they would put a pie and drink on the table for us.

Terri: What do you think is one of the things that today's children don't get that we had growing up in a historically Black community?

Tina: They don't have the influence of our elders and the community, "the village". In those environments, you had family that became friends. They miss that. They don't have that concern where we took care of each other. All of us were poor and lacked physical resources, but we shared what we had with each other and looked out for each other.

Boderick Johnson: Still Crosstown Strong

My name is Boderick Johnson. My mom's name is Maybelle Hicks, but everybody in the neighborhood called her Betty. I have one sister on my mom's side, Delta Stevens; and the neighborhood I grew up in is Crosstown. Crosstown is a well-known part of Gainesville. Growing up, we enjoyed the comradery with other families. The people I grew up with, I still see them around today, and it's good to be able to share memories about that particular part of town.

My fondest memories growing up was spending time at the recreation centers - one was the Wilhelmina Johnson Center across the tracks (across 6th Street) and the other one was the Community Center over on NW 1st St (now Rosa B. Williams Center). As kids, those were our hot spots to hang out and play. More importantly the directors of the programs looked like us and they also ensured that we were well behaved and respectful. So, they were our second parents.

Terri: I remember going to the Center for dances on Friday and sometimes Saturday nights. Did you ever go?

Boderick: Oh absolutely! Those were definitely the hot times right there! Like I said, those are the things that the kids of today's culture just don't get a chance to experience. Those kinds of hanging out or gatherings back then. We didn't worry about kids getting into situations, shooting, fighting, and doing all those types of things because we were having too much fun being around each other. Even when we had disagreements or fights, we didn't hold grudges like that. We didn't wanna kill somebody or get a gun – hell, we didn't even have access to guns. Which was a good thing. We did our thing and the next day we were back with the same person that we had problems with playing football or basketball. We were just like, let bygones be bygones. Yes. Those are the fondest memories I have of growing up in Crosstown.

The Art of Pleasant Street: An Interview with Artist and Storyteller Turbado Marabou

Turbado Marabou is a well-known muralist, storyteller, printmaker, and art teacher. He is also my first love and my husband. Turbado's family lineage and art are an intricate part of Gainesville, and his story is vital in celebrating Gainesville's historically Black communities.

Terri: Please introduce yourself and tell us a little bit about your lineage.

Turbado: Well, my name is Turbado. That is my chosen and given name, but I was born James C. Miller Jr., and my lineage in this community comes from the Cook family and the Miller Davis family. I grew up predominantly in the Cook household, which consists of Altamese Cook and Gaston Troy Cook, Sr. They were the primary caregivers. So yes, when I said Cook, they knew who I was talking about.

We come from a line of teachers and community engagers. I am a third-generation Cook. I'm a PhD candidate, making me a third generation higher education achiever. My grandfather received his PhD out of New York, and my father received his master's and was close to getting his PhD.

My parents are Joyce Cook Miller, and my father was James C. Miller Sr. Both of them grew up here in Gainesville. Growing up, I did not know my father, but I knew my father's family. My mother was a predominantly in-house mother. And she worked jobs here and there. She was a teaching assistant. She was a secretary, things like that. But always in that, you know, the extended family environment was always there.

Everybody knows my dad as Buster. At least a certain generation. It's interesting, when I say you know my daddy, James C. Miller Sr, you know Buster, it was like, "Buster?" It was not a smile, especially from the female acquaintances, it was always like, "Oh, Buster." I'm like, "Oh my God, what did Buster do? What did my father do?" He, to his last breath, never told me what that was and what he did. But he had to leave Gainesville after a certain time.

Terri: So, your family on both sides, are from here in Pleasant Street. Please tell us the name of your paternal grandmother.

Turbado: My paternal grandmother was Saphronia Long. Ma Saphronia is what we knew her by. And then my great-grandmother was Bess Mama. That was my only, real main connection to my father.

Terri: When did your great-grandfather build the house at 710 Northwest 4th Street?

Turbado: My grandfather, well, my great-grandfather was Sam Cook. Sam built that house at the late end of the 20th century, 1898, respectfully. It has been and is still there today. It started out as a humble shotgun house. And then, over time, he built extensions out from that. It was a great deal of property. I'd say really it was about three to four acres that later got reduced.

It pretty much is one of those old-style shotgun houses that we were up on platforms. It was a lot of memories in that house. But Sam was a contractor, and he did a lot of contracting outside of Alachua County. Primarily because outside of Alachua County, nobody knew that he was Black, because Sam passed.

Terri: Passed or passing means that your complexion is so light, almost White, that nobody knows that you are actually of African descent. Was his wife a light-skinned person as well?

Turbado: Absolutely. Fanny was also. I did not know Fanny, but she was very significant in, you know, in the creation of that property in the home. Because there was a house there, and then there was a garage. But the garage had an apartment above it; there were the things of Fanny and Sam's that wound up being in there. And that's when I first saw pictures of her. Fanny had blue eyes and brunette hair. They both passed.

Terri: Tell us about life at 710 and Gaston and Altamese.

Turbado: Well, Gaston was affectionately known as Daddy. That's all we ever called him. Of course, we heard Gaston being called, you know, by my grandmother, right? But everyone said Daddy.

My grandfather had a very interesting history. I only found out later how rich it really was when someone at the University of Florida interviewed him. And he was very much a wanderer.
He loved to travel a lot. Even as a young boy, he would actually just leave and get on the train in the boxcar and go somewhere. He lived in Ocala for a little bit. And he would go in between here and Ocala and other parts of Florida. He actually got adopted by other family members or families he didn't know initially, and he would hang out there. But that's how it was back in the day. You know, there was more of a social connection and certain codes. My grandfather was also very much a man that enjoyed knowledge and the gathering of knowledge.

Growing up, he was the first principal at Williams Elementary, well the Williams Elementary we know now. Back then it was actually a small place on the east side of town right near Lincoln Middle

School. When the new building was built, they literally lined all the kids up and walked them over to the new building. And so that is where he spent most of his career as a principal. He was a teacher for a short minute, but they saw his potential right off the bat and made him a principal.

Prior to that, Daddy attended and was a graduate of Fisk University. And that is where he met my blood grandmother, Mamie Taylor. They wound up going to New York because he was getting his PhD. He was actually Dr. Gaston Troy Cook, Sr., who I had never heard of growing up. He had a small business, he had a coffee shop and a small bookstore there, and they were thriving. He was highly influenced by Dr. W.B. Du Bois. In fact, I have a copy of The Souls of Black Folks with his signature on it that Daddy once owned. But he was called back in this family crisis of his grandfather. Sam and Fannie were getting old. And really, I think it was one of those things that really was the downhill slide for him.

It wasn't soon after that that Mamie got tuberculosis, and she died. She had my uncle, and she still had my mother in her womb when she got tuberculosis. Right after she gave birth, she passed away. It was a very traumatic situation for him. And then he met and married Altamese. (Ma-Mese, affectionately).

So, Ma-Mese was working at Williams Elementary as a teacher. Because we all know about the Union Academy, a lot of the teachers were coming out of Pleasant Street, which is now at the Rosa B Williams Center. She was very effective. She first started out in a one-room schoolhouse. She taught for about 40 - 45 years.

When Mamie passed away, Ma-Mese was not the only one vying for that spot, but it was a few other women in the community were vying to be the next princess. Because he was known as the Prince of the Community. Because he was a Mason. He was an Alpha. He was a principal. And back then, having all those things achieved, you were up to a higher tier. He also owned a small liquor store for a minute. He had a couple of side gigs. He was a volunteer fireman. So, he was highly looked up to as one of the pillars of the community.

Terri: Tell us all about the goings on at 710.

Turbado: I have to say my childhood was really, really cool. You don't know until you look back and see what it really was in terms of the value. My house was one of the main houses that was known as that jugular vein that everyone kind of moved through..

But what was significant for me was how they would have social gatherings there. The Alphas would come there and have meetings, and you would have the Excelsior Matrons, which was a women's social group. That was Altamese's group founded by Mamie. And the majority of Black teachers were there. Then you had the Masons come through.

A lot of educated people and influencers came through. The Chestnuts and the Dukes and so many other people well to do Blacks like, the Cosbys, and the Banks. They would all, at one point, come and pay their respects and socialize in our kitchen or living room. If you were a formal acquaintance, you would be in the living room. You would come in from the front if you didn't know the household like that.

If everybody knew you, you would come into the back and you would pretty much stay in the kitchen. Just hang out. I would observe all these people. Because back then, when you were a child, you were seen, but not heard. But when the old men were having their conversations with my grandfather, I would come in and they would allow me to sit.

And my mother used to tell me, "you know, here you come in like Jesus talking with the rabbis." We were having metaphysical conversations about God and existence, and they allowed me to actually talk, and they would stop and look at me like, Wait a minute. "Gaston, did you tell him that?" And Daddy would answer, "I didn't tell him nothing about it. I think I just rubbed off on him."

You know, I think that's where I got my foundation, not only how to be an intellectual, but also how to be a positive Black man, you know, that was connected and felt an obligation to do good in the community.

Terri: Tell us about 710 and its connection to the Dunbar Hotel.

Turbado: The Dunbar was down the street from us. I remember that it was still active when I was a boy. It wasn't sold until the 80s when, you know, when the whole pervasive selling of property was occurring. But the Dunbar Hotel was a part of that network of safety in terms of space for Black people at that time. The Dunbar was really a great spot where Black celebrities and stars stayed when they performed at the Cotton Club. The Dunbar made sure that visitors were taken care of. It had a very good reputation.

When I was 13 or 14, I remember walking in the back door of 710, and there was BB King, The BB King in the kitchen eating fish and grits with my grandmother. I kind of stood there in shock thinking, *I know you from somewhere and you are famous*. I didn't know a lot about blues, but I had seen enough to know this person was important. Ma-Mese was like, this is my grandson, Jimmy. And he's like, "How are you doing, son? My name is BB King."

I got really starstruck at that point. It turns out that BB King's daughter was being taught by my grandma. And he was coming not only to check on her, but he stopped by to check on us. He made sure he stopped by whenever he was in town and talked to Ma-Mese. Bo Diddley had also come by several times.

The Dunbar had many stars stay there, including all the people on the Chitlin Circuit: James Brown, Muddy Waters, all the greats. It wasn't until later that I actually saw the interior of the actual hotel. It's beautiful in there—absolutely gorgeous. It was also political. Alcee Hastings (the late U.S. Congressman and former judge) came through. The Chestnuts, who owned a funeral home but were also very active in politics here in Gainesville, always came through. They are family. But others who came through were the mucky-mucks at the time. They all had a significant connection with Ma-Mese.

Now my grandfather really just kind of liked certain things. He was more of a recluse. But when people came through, they always made sure they went inside and spoke. They would go to the door of his room and say, "Hey, Gaston, how you doing?" If he really liked you, he would come out. If Daddy came out and sat in the kitchen, it was really a big deal. And man, if they all went in the living room and he pulled out his Wild Turkey Kentucky Bourbon and had some drinks – woo! They would sit in there smoking cigarettes and talking, you know, they're having a good time.

There was a really rich connection to 710 in terms of music and politics. These famous people kept their humility and stayed connected to the community, you know, knowing what was important, and that kind of stayed with me.

Terri: Speaking of humility, please tell the story of when your sister Pam and your cousin lost you at Publix.

Turbado: That is a significant story. It is traumatizing for my sister and my cousin, but it was I'm a "big boy" significant for me. The big kids were going somewhere, and I wanted to go too. Back then, even during that time of the segregation transition, you could still walk, you know, with a chaperone. My sister and my cousin were going to the Gainesville Shopping Center, where there was Belks, there was Publix, a toy store, and a pet store. There were two things I definitely loved to go to: the toy store and the pet store.

My sister was like, "No. I'm not going to take you."

My grandmother was like, "Take your brother."

So we went, and they're doing the usual thing. "Don't talk." "Don't do this." You know, they were giving me the lines of things that I shouldn't do. And I was like three or four. So, we were there, and then they decided they had to go to the bathroom at the same time, and they told me, "You stay right here. Don't you move. Don't you talk to anybody. You understand?"

And I was like, "OKAY!" I can't imagine what my face was like. Probably more like.
Really? I was very fast thinking, still am, but, you know, really quick thinking and vengeful at that age. So they went into the bathroom, and I was like I'll show them. So, I walked out of the shopping center. I think this is where my sense of direction really started and solidified. I began to walk home. Now, imagine a four-year old who understood how to cross the street. People stopped as I crossed 8th Avenue.

When I got home, my grandma was like, "Where Pam and Donnie?"

I told her, "They're at the store. They left me to go to the bathroom."

She asked, "So you walked home all by yourself?"

And I said all proud, "Yes!"

So, I'm sitting there eating this nice bowl of doobie and drinking a glass of milk. And I'm looking out the window, and there's Donnie and Pam running down the street. Grandma was like, "Shh, shh, shh, don't say nothing."

Grandma asks them when they come in, "Where's Jimmy?""

They didn't say nothing.

"I don't see Jimmy. You lost that baby? You better go back to that store and find Jimmy."

They burst into tears! (laughing) They went running back to the shopping center, wailing and flailing. They came back about 15 or 30 minutes later, and I was sitting on the porch swinging my legs back and forth, smiling. They both looked at me. If death had a stare, that was it. At that moment, they looked at me, and the tears turned into anger. They were huffing and puffing.

And Grandma told them, "You can look at him like that, but you better not tell him nothing and you better not try to hit him either. You know you shouldn't have left him. He's four years old." And she went through the whole nine yards. Pam and Donnie got a spanking that day. Donnie got an extra spanking that day. I always got Donny in trouble! They did get me back though, a few times over.

But it was a paramount moment for me. I think that's why I had a sense of independence. I definitely knew how to think on my feet, and I realized the power of a child is invincible if you know how to use it.

Terri: As long-time residents of Pleasant Street, we grew up in our parents' houses, which were basically connected to each other. How do you feel about gentrification? Does it affect you?

Turbado: I'm a little bit more traumatized. I think that trauma was manifested back in the 80s, 90s, as I was still in school, I remember starting to see activity that I couldn't identify. Strange young men on the corner, people knocking on your door, asking for items, and not coming back with them, flashlights, a dollar, And you're like, "What the heck is going on? What is this?" And that's when I noticed there was a change happening in the community.

It wasn't long after that, in the 90s, that people started selling their homes. It wasn't obvious at first, but people started abandoning their homes, moving out east or somewhere else and never returning. They would go up north or go to another larger city. That was really the first start of it.

The real point of trauma for me was when my grandmother had just passed away. My grandfather had already passed away back in the 80s. It's important for people to understand the vastness of property that we once owned. We had property in Alachua. We had property all around Pleasant Street. So, at one time, one-third of Gainesville, was owned by Black people and our family had a significant amount. One family member even owned property out where Oaks Mall is now.

So, at the time, I was in my first marriage, and I returned home to Gainesville, and got a job as a teacher. They had just started building new homes over here in Pleasant Street.

First, my uncle, or my grandmother, sold the property that was where your house is now, where your Mom bought her house. That was all our property. Where all those little shotgun houses were back there on NW 5th Street. I remember the turmoil of my grandmother's death started, and then I found out that my uncle was going to sell the house. My great-grandfather built that house. My grandfather didn't buy the house, he and then my uncle inherited the house. I was in line to inherit it too.

When I asked to buy the house, he said, without hesitation, "You can't afford it."

So even though I was mad, my upbringing kicked in, and I said, "I don't understand, sir."

But in the back of my head, I was like, afford what? You didn't buy that house. So why are you telling me I can't afford it?

And so, the mentality of that is what I talk about and try to teach to this day—the problem of Heirs Property. You have family members who you trust as elders, and you get betrayed by them, and they cut your inheritance off. The opportunity for me to have my ancestral home, where I grew up, where all my experiences were, was completely cut off.

Then, items that belonged to my grandmothers, my blood one and the one I was raised by, Ma Mese, and all the things inside that belonged to Daddy, were distributed to other family members. And I got a ring. It was a ring from my grandmother that I had bought her, and that ring represented, for me, the betrayal.

I buried that ring with her. I just said, "You can have it back." The trauma of that is long-lasting, to the point that I continue to have issues about buying property for myself, based on the fact that in my heart, I felt like I deserved not to have to buy the house. I deserved that house I was raised in. It was a legacy of ownership and entitlement that I was denied.

I had done everything that the family asked me to do. And so, you know, having an MFA, teaching, never being in jail, never embarrassing you, married - the whole nine yards! I did the best I could.

And so, to betray that pact, to betray that tradition is what got me into that state of just, you know, I don't know if you call it victimization or self-imposed victimization. I feel like if I can't have that house, then I won't have anything.

In my final attempt to get the house, when things shifted financially, I had seen it priced at $250,000. All my ducks were in a row, and I was again in a position to buy the house from the people who had lived there. And we knew them well. Ann, the owner, found a picture of my grandmother there. She and I took it as a sign, you know, that I could do it. But she had to sell it before I could get it from her. But I kept saving and when I was ready, gentrification reared its ugly head. The house went from $250,000 to $425,000. I was in shock.

Terri: Not only is it not yours, but we are also seeing White people living in that house and remembering when they absolutely wouldn't even walk down the street.

Turbado: Exactly. They never would come to that side of the street ever. And so now in our neighborhood, on our street where we both grew up, our side of the street that we live on right now are African-Americans, and on the side of the street where 710 is, which is across the street from us, are all White people. There are no Black families on that side of the street.

Fortunately, some young people have acquired the Dunbar Hotel on that side of the street. So, at least, there will be some Black people in the Dunbar.

Terri: One of Gainesville's activists, Sharon Burney, says gentrification is violent.

Turbado: I agree with Sharon. It is a violent, violent thing because it hurts us deeply. I'd rather you hit me. I can repair that. It (gentrification) hurts us on the deepest levels, right in the heart.

GAINESVILLE PROPER

21. **Sam and Fannie Cook House   circa 1895**
Sam and Fannie Cook built this house and a small store on land purchased from Ella and Lawrence Davis, just south of Fannie's brother, Jennings Feltner. Feltner, together with N. M. Clinton and Irwin Haynes, founded the first volunteer fire company and served as City Tax Assessor, 1888-1889. Gaston T. Cook, Sr., son of

GAINESVILLE PROPER

PORTERS QUARTERS

Porters Quarters is one of Gainesville's oldest historically-Black neighborhoods. It was established in 1884 by Canadian physician, Dr. Watson Porter. The neighborhood was named after Porter and his wife, Olivia, who divided the land around Porter Street, which is now SW 5th Street. The Porters created the area as a Black settlement that gave residents access to jobs in downtown Gainesville.

The neighborhood's oldest church, Shady Grove Primitive Baptist Church, was organized in 1894 and still stands, although in a new building.

Just like its close neighbor, Pleasant Street, Porters Quarters is a victim of gentrification.

Community activists such as Faye Williams continue to fight for not only the preservation of the culture of Porters but for development that benefits the residents. The activists of Porters Quarters work hard to encourage its citizens to be vocal about their desire to stay authentic, and their determination to keep their history intact while creating a sustainable future for the children growing up there.

Two programs that demonstrate Porters Quarters' commitment to self-advocacy and determination are Porters Quarters Community Farm and the Porters Quarters Freedom School. Both offer residents the opportunity to participate in activities that nurture residents, young and old.

Replaced But Not Erased: Fighting The Displacement of Black Residents in Gainesville's Historically Black Neighborhoods

We are seeing lifelong residents of our beloved communities being erased and replaced by student housing, professionals who love the quaintness of older Black communities, and home buyers who look nothing like the people who settled and have occupied the areas for more than a century. My neighborhood is a perfect example of this phenomenon. Pleasant Street is the oldest African American settlement in Gainesville, Florida. I have seen the destruction of my community firsthand as our historic mix of beautiful and historic shotgun houses and old-style Queen Anne and Colonial homes have been replaced. Many of the newer constructed dwellings are used for student housing and Airbnb-type rentals, changing the authentic culture of the neighborhood, making it inhospitable for the indigenous residents. Disrespectful development has even touched churches. In the picture below, an Airbnb was built right up to the church's back door, with no consideration for worshipers' ability to park for Sunday services.

At a 2023 community planning meeting for Sarah's Sweetwater Greenway Loop Festival that celebrated Gainesville's historic neighborhoods, former (and a few current) residents of historically Black communities discussed how our neighborhoods no longer felt familiar or safe. In contrast, White residents who now live in those communities stated how they moved into the neighborhoods, not only because of their proximity to the University of Florida and downtown but also because of the welcoming community feel many of them had never experienced. The very feeling that attracted them to the neighborhood was no longer accessible to lifelong residents with ancestral ties. They didn't understand how or why we felt so disconnected.

"Most of these African American communities, all of them, have been marginalized and left behind historically. It's very easy to see the disparity."

**Gainesville City Commissioner Desmon Walker,
Independent Alligator article, Revisiting Porters Quarters: The Ongoing Challenge with Gentrification (2024)**

TERRI L. BAILEY, MA

Thank You Sistah Desmon

With a spirit of love for our community
Sis you move so effortlessly and quite deliberately
Through Crosstown and out East
But if need be
You will articulately
Raise hell in Haile
And then gracefully
Take a seat at the head of the table
Like you own it

With brown legs crossed at the knee
You skillfully define
Some mess sneakily designed
To diminish our shine
And in a voice most polite you say
No sir, not today
While brushing thick hair from almond eyes
You clear your view so you can spy
And ensure today there will be no demise
Of our community

Sis I see you
Working on the front line
And behind the scenes
Preventing their ability to diminish or demean
Our institutions and our icons
Preserving our memories before they're all gone
That ain't gone happen because here we stand strong
Firmly rooted in the knowledge that right here's where we belong
Historically and eternally tethered to this soil

Yes, they tried to beat you down
They must not know 'bout that Gainesville Green
Thought taking away your title
Would run you off the scene
The laughs on them you see
Cuz you still out here manifesting dreams
Bringing vision to fruition while speaking power over these streets
They discounted that survivor DNA
That came from ancestors who were once enslaved

But are now free to breathe that warrior fire through the veins of you and me
HAHA! I bet they know now!

Girl we glad to have you back at home
This town sho needed your voice
And on this election day
I just pray
Folks make the right choice
But regardless of the outcome
Gainesville has already won
Because you boldly took a stand
For the people's needs and our demands
And regardless of where you stand
Be it on the dais
Or down on Duncan land
Because of your efforts together we band
Fighting purposely for our lives and united in love

Thank you, Sistah Desmond! We sho 'preciate you!

Ase!

The Things Family Teaches You!
Tonia Potter

Terri: Please say your name, your lineage, and what neighborhood you are representing.

Tonia: My name is Tonia Potter. My lineage is the Thomases, Alice Thomas; and I grew up in Porters Quarters.

Terri: Tell me what was great about growing up in a historically Black community and give me one of your favorite childhood memories.

Tonia: What was so great about growing up in a historically Black community was that we all were family. We all took care of each other, and we grew up, and we learned from the elders in our community; we really did.

One of my fondest memories would be trying out for cheerleading and *my grandmother* literally teaching me how to do a split; and her watching me. Also singing on the porch with her every day. Those are a couple of my fondest memories about being in Porters. And the others passing by who I went to school with and walking to school with me from there.

Terri: That's so great! So, your grandmother taught you how to do a split? Did you make the team?

Tonia: I was hurting, but I made it! She rubbed me down every day, but I did that split.

Porters Quarters, A Wonderful Place for Imagination
Darryl King

My name is Darryl King, and I'm from Porters Quarters. My family is the Perkins family. They moved into Porters from Monteocha, FL. My grandmother and my grandfather moved down from Monteocha first. My grandmother was a Brown before she married my granddaddy, who was a Perkins. My parents' names were Peter King and Dolly King. My grandparents were Lucille Perkins and George Perkins.

We're also related to the Leath family, and we're related to the Simmons family, the Williams family (that's also in Porters), and Miss Janie Williams.

Growing up in Porters was a lot of fun! Back then, we played outside all the time. We had a group called the Porters Rangers and that was a bunch of us kids that lived in the Porters. We would go down to the park, and we would play down there all day long. We would play in the creek. We played basketball. One rule about the Porters Rangers was you couldn't go home until they said you could go home, so we were down there all day.

We played softball in the park. We played basketball at the park. Back then, they used to have a big Army tank that was there, so we used to play in the tank and all kinds of stuff. Up in the woods, there was a big creek that ran through there, and we used to go down there and get sharks' teeth. On the other side, further up in the woods, there was a big opening, and they called it some kind of swimming hole, but we never got into it because it was too deep.

Tumblin Creek Park was on the other side. That same creek that ran through Porters ran through Tumblin Creek. And it was on the other side of the road. It wasn't called Tumblin Creek in Porters, but on the other side, they called it Tumblin Creek.

Some people didn't know there was another park up in Porters. But it was. We had a big field. Now if you go through Porters, you'll see where they have the big retention pond. My grandmother's old house, their first house, was over where that retention pond is. There were a lot of other houses over there. There was a dirt road that cut through and went down to where the church is at (I don't know the name of it now). It used to be owned by Pastor Dennison; they bought that church. Now they built a lot of apartments over there, but down from there, there was an entrance that we used to go through; the path is what we called it. We used to go through that way, to cut through going all the way to the back, and that's where the deep swimming hole was. We would go back there and play. We spent a lot of time just running around, having a good time.

Peter King: We Never Knew We Were Poor Because We Were Rich With Community

I am Peter King, and I grew up in Porters Quarters in the Southwest part of Gainesville - SW 6th St. and 5th Ave., right by the railroad tracks. My grandmother and grandfather are George and Lucille Perkins from the Porters side (that's on my maternal side). On my paternal side would be Beatrice and John King, Sr., and my dad who is Peter King, is a junior. His given name is John Henry King, Jr, and his nickname is Peter. That's where I got my name from. I'm little Peter. My mother is Pastor Dolly, or Prophetess Dolly King. We're all from the Porters area and also by way of Monteocha. I have one sibling. His name is Darrell King. He is also from Porters Quarters. We were raised up together and we all went to PK Young together.

One of the things that sticks out for me growing up in Porters Quarters is you never knew that you were poor. Our families, like my grandmother's sister, the Leaths, lived around the corner, and we all grew up like brothers and sisters. In that neighborhood, we were always being looked out for by other adults in the community. If you got in trouble around the area or by a neighborhood house, that rolled around to your house. You got disciplined over there, and you got disciplined when you got home. So, where it says it takes a village to raise a child is actually true, and that's what was going on when I was growing up. We couldn't run from the trouble. Well, not trouble, but from that punishment.

I look at it today and think about the community and how it's changed. At one point in time, nobody wanted to cross the railroad tracks, but now everything is growing to the east. They stopped pushing through the West, and now they're sucking up our communities. Things are turning more Caucasian. They're taking houses and making it harder to build housing in our own areas, our own neighborhoods, which is tough. We don't have the finances, we don't have the resources, and a lot of us don't have the jobs (needed) in order to buy and build the houses they're now requiring you to put in these neighborhoods, which is disheartening.

But my fondest memories are about growing up and playing in the neighborhood 'til it gets dark; playing roly poly, hide and go seek, calling chicki chicken nobi while playing hide and go seek. You know all those things, but growing up as a family, with my friends, in Porters is one of the most priceless things to me. Nobody plays outdoors anymore, and you can't run around like that anymore. But I love Porters Quarters, and I thank God for it.

Henry Leath – My Life is a Musical

My name is Henry William Leath III. I'm the grandson of Seroy Leath and Rebecca Whitaker. My mother's name is Maddie Peoples Leath, and my father's name is Henry William Leath II. I've never met my mother's father or even seen a picture of him. He died when my mother was at a young age.

I'm representing downtown Porters Quarters. I grew up over here. My mother and father grew up over here too. They were homeowners. My grandfather ran a cleaner (dry cleaning store) over here. I don't remember the name of it. My mother was raised by a single mother who had four girls and three boys. One of her sons was killed in the Korean War, one committed suicide, and one went into the Navy. All the girls went to college. My mother went to Fort Valley State. My aunt Nelly went to Tuskegee Institute. and my other aunt, Atlene went to Florida Memorial, and the youngest, Betty Cobb, went to Florida A&M.

I was around educators. I grew up in Porters, and I had an awesome childhood. I can't remember too many traumatic incidents - other than I experienced seeing people who had been shot a couple of times. Other than that, there were really no traumatic incidences growing up over in this neighborhood.

I always say my life was a musical because we lived around the corner from what was called a juke joint. They were called that because they had jukeboxes. Once they opened, you could hear music all over the neighborhood from opening until closing, which was like 12:00 at night. So, the popular songs I can place to events. You know? I always tell people my life was a musical because it was always music playing.

The neighborhood was close-knit, and it was a working-class neighborhood. On Fridays, the men went to the neighborhood bar and did whatever they did. The weekends were great for me. Saturday was me and my mother's day. We went riding often. We went shopping and went around, you know. Until I turned 12 or 13, and kind of cut her loose. She was heartbroken, but I got older.

I'm the only boy - I have three older sisters. Mother and Father spent a good portion of their lives before I was born in New York City. My daddy worked up there for about seven years. And my mother carried me there for like eight months. They were living in Bed-Stuy Brooklyn on Halsey Street. So, when they came back here, they had a different attitude from the other Southerners as far as the way they were raising kids and stuff like that. We called our mother and father by their first names. I got in trouble a lot because I wasn't used to saying "ma'am", and "yes sir", and that type of thing when I went to people's houses. That stood out. I would always get corrected.

My mother always exposed me to a lot. Anything that I took interest in, she fostered it and supported it. She exposed me to a lot of different things. I remember in 1972, they had a sit-in in front of Tigert Hall, which turned into a little riot. I was curious about it, so me and my mother (after it kind of died down), rode through there. I remember two students picked up a big bus stop bench with bricks and ran across the street with it and put it right in front of our car. You know that was exciting for me.

Like I said, my life was a musical. My sisters were into music. They had racks of 45s. Like every album that came out. I remember my biggest thing was reading the album covers. I couldn't wait until they bought a new album just to read the album cover and the inside. You know, it was like a book. The cover told a lot about all the band members, and that was really exciting for me.

My mother used to have me tagging along with my sisters everywhere, and they didn't like that. I got a lot of resentment from my sisters which they still carry to this day. I understand why my mother did that, because they were girls, and I (for lack of a better word), I was the cockblocker.

But that was cool because once we got where we were going, I was free to go do what I wanted to do. You know they got rid of me. So, every event, I was there. I had two sisters who were cheerleaders. We were fortunate to go to PK Young in the ninth grade. My whole family on my Father's side, for the most part, went there. His brother's children grew up down the street from us. He had eight children, and they lived four houses down from us. We were really close.

When I think about children growing up now in Porters Quarters, one thing that sticks out is we had like party wars. That's what I call them. Everyone tried to outdo everybody with a birthday party. You went to everybody's birthday party, whether you wanted to go or not. The kids now, they're lacking basic respect. Because growing up in Black neighborhoods (in previous years) you got chastised by anybody. If you were doing wrong, cussing, or whatever, if someone heard you, they would beat your behind and tell your mama and your daddy. You know that basic respect thing. They demanded kids be respectful. I didn't know then, but you know, kids came from families that didn't really instill that, but even so, the neighborhood raised those kids.

There were a lot of families that pretty much took on kids, like adopted kids, if mothers weren't good mothers. They would just take care of the kids and raise them as their own. There was a lot of that. They took them as their own. There's not much of that going on these days. But all the kids were taken care of and protected. We were allowed to be children. We didn't worry about anyone messing with us because if they messed with us, a person could get killed over here back then. All the incidents of kids being abducted and sexual abuse now, if folks found out a person did that over here back then, they would have gotten messed up. You really didn't mess with the kids. Yeah, that was off limits.

So, we were able to be children. We would do children's things. And the ones that stepped out and crossed that line, they heard the word Mariana. Mariana was like the boys home.

[Interviewer's note: Mariana was a notorious reformatory school. Many people in the neighborhood would say those sent there didn't come back, and if they did, they didn't come back right mentally or behaviorally.]

Yep. Well, we moved into this house in 1981. We renovated this house, me and my father. That's one thing that I feel pride for, because my father and I worked on this house after school. After practice, I would come up here to help my father, and you know I took a lot of pride in doing that. We moved in when we got back from the tournament. We were playing basketball at PK, and we just came from the state basketball tournament. We played in the championship game, and we got beat. I went to the old house where we stayed by the railroad track. We were the last house right before you got to the park. I went there, and the house was empty, and I was like, "Wow, he's moved!" I didn't have a room. Back then, most of these houses over here were two-bedroom houses, and you had families with ten people living in two-bedroom houses, but everyone was happy. We didn't know we were all poor. If a family didn't have, people helped out that family. If you had a three-bedroom house, we thought you were kind of well off.

People had a lot of success stories from Porters. We had a lot of tragedies, but it's still home. For the most part, most of the people that grew up over here really made something of themselves because it was a thing to want to leave and do better. You know, go away and do better. Kids don't have that now. It was a desire when you got out of high school you wanted to leave, to go off and spread your wings. You know kids don't have that desire to do that anymore.

Porters Quarters Hidden Folk Art Treasure: Alyne Harris

Alyne Harris is a renowned self-taught folk artist from Gainesville, Florida, born in 1942. She is known for her paintings that highlight Black spirituality, nature, and Black life down South. The scenes often include memories from her childhood. Her works, which are vibrant and colorful, reflect her unique vision of the world around her.

Harris' art has been showcased in various notable exhibitions, including:

- American Folk Art Museum in New York
- Gainesville's Thomas Center Galleries, where she has held several exhibitions celebrating her life's work.
- High Museum of Art in Atlanta, which has displayed her pieces in exhibitions featuring Southern self-taught artists.

This interview was conducted one Friday evening from her front porch in Porters Quarters.

My name is Alyne Harris. My mama's name was Miss Bertha Harris, but some of them called her Bell. But Bell was her nickname. And my daddy's name is Otis Harris, and then my half-brother was named after him – Li'l Otis.

Terri Bailey: Share the story with us about your uncle who had to leave Lake City.

Alyne Harris: He had to leave Lake City because he got in some trouble about whopping a White guy. I don't know what happened. Mama was seven years old when it happened. The Masons got him out of there that night - they took him all the way to Plant City, but they had to hide him until they put him on a train all the way to Jacksonville. They had to dress him up another way (disguise him).

The Klan come looking for him, but he wasn't there. My grandma said, "He's gone, and we don't know where he was." He headed north and that's how he got to Milwaukee and that's where he stayed.

Mama was just a girl comin' up, but she told me that happened. Yep, when we got grown he told us "I whooped that man's ass! I whooped that cracker" and everything like that. And I said, "Uncle Sylvester, what he done?" He ain't never say.

It was bad here. My mama said, Newberry was a lynching place. They hung a woman there in Newberry, I heard about it a long time ago. I don't remember it though, somebody told me. They said the maid dropped a baby, but the maid said she didn't have no baby. She was there to clean the house and cook. But they said the maid did it and hung her on a tree and split her down the middle.

And you take Rosewood down there wasn't no better - that's not too far from Rawlings, Florida. It was terrible. That's just the way it was.

Terri: Have you always lived in Porters?

Ms. Harris: I lived out there by the graveyard when we were children coming up. Then we moved into town after my grandmama passed away. We lived there on 12th Street (Cross Town). And then later on, when they started building houses over there in Porters Quarters, Joel Buchanan was telling everybody they could move over there.

I was working for Ms. Ethel. Ms. Ethel was a mean, hateful White landlady - she didn't like to fix stuff in the houses.

He said they would be building houses over in Porters. He told us to go to class about how to become a homeowner and get one of the new houses. So, I went to class, and I got a big ol' house over here (Porters). My sister wanted me to move over here before she passed away. She was glad that I moved over here. I've been here I'd say, for about 19 years.

Terri: I'm interested to know how it was living over in Porters before gentrification.

Ms. Harris: Well, I tell you what, you had a juke over here and stuff like that. Yeah, they used to call it a Bucket of Blood and the Sweet Water Branch; it was a long time ago.

There were houses over here. Mr. Cope had houses over here. I guess he's dead and gone. Him and Beasley Williams, he's dead and gone too. I remember Beasley Williams and I remember Mr. Cope.

Terri: Miss Alyne, did you go to the Bucket of Blood and to the other dances and stuff?

Ms. Harris: No, I didn't go. I didn't go to them dances. But they had Ike's place.

People just went there to juke. My cousin's husband ran the pool hall. But he's dead and gone now. And it was another place; I can't remember the name. I pass it every day, but I have to look up the name of it. Some of them went to that place and all that and juke. And they used to juke all night long. And all of them old songs at 5th Avenue. It was another tavern and Dorothy Kendell was there. And there was Fletcher's place down there. I was 14 years old. And there was Mom's Kitchen. I don't know if it came later. But I remember those days. I said, "Okay, I'd like to go hear the blues and stuff like that."

Terri: Where'd you go to hear the blues?

Ms. Harris: Well, I hear them. I mean, you could hear the blues anywhere. I used to get my hair done and sit in the chair and hear 'Darlin' You Send Me'. All that. Yes, James Brown, Nat King Cole, and all like that. We had all of them old songs. Yes and Reverend Cato - he had a drug store down there. The only burgers I liked was Reverend Cato burgers. He had the best burgers.

Well, I made my money by working for the schoolteacher. I made 'bout $15. When Mama says, "I'm not going to cook." I would buy me a burger at Cato. I had my nephew too, so I would have a bag full of hot dogs and hamburgers. Cato used to give me extra stuff in it. And honey, them hamburgers was so good!

I remember Mr. Robinson's store. Mama used to go down to Mr. Robinson's store all the time. That was downtown. Some people used to dress up and go down there. Mama wore her tennis shoes and dress down there.

Dorothy Kendell used to do my hair and that's where I would hear a lot of music. And then there was little Clara, down from Dorothy. I remember little Clara. I remember those people plain as day.

And I remember Duncan Brothers Funeral Home and stuff like that. Lord, people used to clown down there (on 5th Avenue). And then Sergeant Lewis used to walk up down the street and look at who he could put in jail. He liked to show out in front of the White people up there. Just show out. And I remember Cubie during that time. Cat wrote Cubie. Miss Mary Scott wrote Cubie. It was a guy, they called him Rip, he would go and tell who was writing Cubie. And my aunt grabbed Rip by the collar one day and said, "You better not tell on my friends down there! " But he did. He told on Mary Scott and got her husband put in jail. And he didn't know what he did. The White guy who they was writing Cubie for told her don't worry about it. They tell me they burned Rip up in the house one night. He was drunk when he got burned up in the house, and nobody talked about it no more.

Cubie is playing the numbers. And now it's just called lottery. Mama used to play a five-nine-one. I told my son Troy; I dreamed about my mama last night. I said, "I can get a five-nine-one – that number coming." I said, "You ought to go out and get it and get you a beer!" Yeah, Mama used to play that number five-nine-one. That was her number. She would call over to the night house and say, "What's going on?" I don't remember what they paid when it hit back then. You know, a hundred-dollar or something like that, but I think they paid a dollar for it. I remember when Mama played at Cat's near her apartment, and Mama caught that number. I never will forget that.

Terri: Miss Harris, did you ever know Jesse Aaron, who was an artist?

Ms. Harris: I used to be around him a lot. Yeah, he was really nice man. His wife is some kin to my mama. I would be around there, putting cookies in a jar for her and stuff like that. She would give me my lunch money. Mama fixed me them peanut butter and jelly sandwiches, and I'd throw them in the 12th Street branch. I didn't let nobody see because people would tell on you back in them days.

Terri: We used to go hang out with Mr. Jesse. All of us kids regret throwing away the little things that Mr. Aaron would help you sculpt and do that whittling stuff, make little sculptures out of pieces of wood. Now all of us wish we would have kept that stuff, because it would be worth some money, wouldn't it?

Ms. Harris: Yes, the wooden things. He's passed and I think both his daughters are gone now. They done died out. The house is torn down, but they (the City) should have made it a historic house. I guess ain't nobody think about it. They just sold it, and they got other buildings there now.

Terri: Me and my husband went to cultural affairs and talked to them about purchasing that house from the family and making it a historical site. But they didn't do it.

Ms. Harris: Yeah, they could have done it. Just like they did Mr. Jones house over there. I remember that building used to be old Lincoln High School. I remember them days.

I went to old Lincoln High School, and I went to new Lincoln. I remember it was an elementary school there too. And Mrs. Lane - boy, she was a mean teacher. Everybody thought I was Mrs. Lane's pick. She always had me pass out the papers. She said, "Girl, your mama cooked good cakes." Tell her to cook me a cake and things like that.

One boy's mama came in and told Miss Lane, "If my son don't get his work, you have my permission to tear him up." She whooped that boy on every round. She came up there with that paddle. If he got his numbers wrong, she's whooping. If he got his spelling wrong, she's whooping. All that boy got was a paddle, boy that Mrs. Lane was something else.

Terri: Tell me, what do you miss about the old Porters?

Ms. Harris: The old Porters? Okay. Now, Ike place was over there. And there was Black gal she used to work right over with Ike. Now, she could cook some good livers and gizzards. I used to go over there and get some and come back here to the house. I miss that. You know, Ike's daughter, after he died, said she wasn't going to keep it because she said she wasn't going to be able to pay tax on that.

She sold to the city because it was too much money for her to pay tax. She got her a home in Stone Mountain, Georgia.

There was another place called a club somewhere. People used to go to the jukebox there.

Terri: At the Cotton Club?

Ms. Harris: Yeah, the Cotton Club. Boy they used to boogie, boogie there. I knew a lady, she's gone now. She said, "You should go to the Cotton Club and boogie, boogie, boogie."

Terri: Miss Alyne, how long have you been painting?

Ms. Harris: I've been painting for about 20 odd years now. A long time. I started from The 5th Avenue Art Show (The 5th Ave Arts Festival). You know Nkwanda was over that show, she started that show. Yes, I started right at the 5th Avenue show. I love to paint the woods and stuff like that and the old-time houses and wildflowers and angels and stuff like that. That's my favorite thing to do.

TERRI L. BAILEY, MA

GAINESVILLE PROPER

Mr. Scherwin Henry is a scientist, educator, musician, politician and more. In 2005, he helped open a Bethune Cookman College extension site at Eastside High School in Gainesville, Florida. Although the program was short lived, 90% of the students that started graduated with honors.

For the Love of Mr. Henry

One day God appeared to you
And said, Scherwin I have a plan
I need you to complete a task for me
That my daughter Mary began

Don't worry about your ability
Because I gave you a great foundation
I'll supply the rest of the things you need
To add to my great nation

You have the strength and discipline
That you got from Momma Altamese
And just like your daddy Pop Henry
Many hungry minds you'll feed

With the grace of your Auntie Barbara
You will nurture and make them believe
That with faith in their creator
Great things can be achieved

Now go and build a mighty team
To help you on this mission
Look to those close to you
That will see the total vision

You enlisted the help of Mrs. Henry
A pioneer in education
Dean Jackie Polke brought to the team
Practicality and strong determination

Ms. V. contributed a watchful eye
And a talent for organization
With the team's completion you began the task
Of building the student population

One by one you sought us out
And led us to BCU
You showed us how to erase the doubt
And how God would see us through

You encountered some issues and some mess
Compliments of the enemy
But you brushed them off and did not stress 'Cause you were a part of God's mighty team

As we each complete our programs
And see the fulfillment of our dreams
Each and every one of us
Are forever a part of this team

When we enter the world to begin our tasks
And fulfill our destinies
We will keep in our minds, our hearts, and souls
Love and thanks for Mr. Henry

SPRINGHILL

The Springhill neighborhood has roots going back to the early 20th century. It was established during segregation to provide a safe and welcoming community for Black residents who faced systemic discrimination in housing, education, and employment. Over time, the neighborhood also became known as a cultural and social hub. Most notable is Sarah McKnight's Cotton Club, which welcomed blues greats like James Brown, BB King, Bo Diddley, and Ray Charles.

Families living in Springhill formed local businesses that helped sustain the neighborhood economically. In its early years, the neighborhood was self-sufficient, with grocery stores, barbershops, beauty salons, and other businesses owned and operated by Black entrepreneurs.

Over the decades, however, Springhill faced many of the challenges that impacted Black neighborhoods nationwide, such as underinvestment, limited access to resources, and threats from urban renewal policies. As Gainesville grew, development pressures and gentrification began to reshape Springhill, pushing some long-time residents out and altering the fabric of the community. Despite these challenges, Springhill remains a significant part of Gainesville's Black history and identity, with residents and advocates working to preserve its legacy and protect its future.

GAINESVILLE PROPER

The Rebirth of Gainesville's Cotton Club

Come on y'all let's celebrate
The rebirth of the Cotton Club
Back in the day it was first rate
Filled with music, laughter, and love

Its walls hold our rich history
And tells the story of Black life
It disproves the myths and theories
That our world was just struggle and strife

This building was once our theater
Showing images reflecting our own
It was the property of the Perryman's
Here the top race films were shown

The McKnights who we all know
Put the club on the Chittlin' Circuit
Blacks from all parts would come and show
Musical skills that we'd never forget

Blues greats like BB King
Performed in this small town
And when soul became the song to sing
The Cotton Club brought in James Brown

We danced to the latest grooves
We dressed up and came to show out
Gainesville's finest showed off their moves
And their coolest threads no doubt

The soldiers who came home on leave
We welcomed with a warm embrace
We'd congratulate the things they achieved
With a pride not clouded by race

When the music stopped, and the lights went dim
The Cotton Club closed its doors
Its heyday a faded memory to them
Who shucked and jived across its floors

Just like the sphinx standing strong and still
Its shell neglected and worn
Sistah Filer & the board found the way and the will
For the Cotton Club to be reborn

Its gonna take our entire community
Giving money, time and more
Gainesville must show much unity
For the Cotton Club to be restored

We owe it to our parents,
Their parents, ourselves, and our seed
The rebirth of this great establishment
Is a noble cause indeed

Once more the Cotton Club will shine
Hosting artists and musicians galore
Culture itself will be redefined
With the opening of its doors

So put up the posters and send out the call
Our very best clothes we'll adorn
Oh, what a good time will be had by all
Cuz the Cotton Club has been reborn!

We Will Never Know Where We've Been Unless We Tell The Story
Professor Emerita Vivian Lee Washington Filer

Mrs. Vivian Filer is a major influence in my life. She is a storyteller, community advocate, and community mother. In fact, in 2023, she was given the title Queen Mother Mangye Naa Amiami Osuowaa Okropong I.

I've always felt a special connection to her and have studied closely how she moves through the world, effortlessly giving out love, lessons, and discipline to community members, young and old. I recently found out about another connection to this beloved elder. Miss Karen, who was my favorite babysitter when I was little, is her sister. The only time Miss Karen ever got angry with me was when I refused to finish a bowl of oatmeal that she made for me. Whenever I see her, I tell her how much I love her and that I'm going to finish that bowl of oatmeal. Although she has long since forgotten that forty-year-old incident. She always smiles, hugs me, and tells me how proud she is of me. The community mothering gene must be in their DNA.

I absolutely love them both and am so appreciative that Mangyne took the time out of her busy schedule to share about her life, her neighborhood, and her family.

I lived most of the time that I've been in Gainesville - in the Springhill neighborhood - that's Springhill as, one word and not two. When they built that new place northwest, they named it Spring Hill. But we are the Springhill neighborhood. The southeast side of town.

I'm the co-founder of the Springhill Neighborhood Association or neighborhood watch. And what I found was that there were parameters that we hadn't really been defined very well. We have a narrower definition now of what it was originally. You know, Main Street is the center of town. If you go in one direction, your east all the way to your west. If you're east of Main Street, we'll start at Main Street and go all the way up to Waldo Road. And that would be our east west corridor. And on the north side we would start at Fourth Avenue and go over to 10th Avenue.

So that block in there - and I know that's defined narrowly now by us, but we did that as we developed the neighborhood watch because there were other neighborhoods developing around there and calling themselves different things. And so, from 10th Street over, that becomes Sugar Hill, and that's why we made that separation.

In older days, I loved that the neighbors all felt as if they were co-owners of all the children, . But the fact is, if you had an elder present and a child was involved, everybody knew that elder was in charge. And that was a natural understanding because we had to trust all of the parents to raise all of the children. We knew that collectively we were their protectors. They, the older ones, were our protectors, because outside of our Black world, there were very many dangerous places that they could be and things to do.

If you were in a Black community, you could depend on help being there. Where my mother worked, at the College Inn, which was called the CI, was there on University Avenue. Many blocks, of course, was Smathers Library, that little shopping area there; in the middle of that was a College Inn. And to date it, it was back in the time when Steve Spurrier was playing football. My mother always talked about feeding him there.

But my mother worked there and walked from there to Springhill after she finished work, sometimes after eight in the evening. And my sisters and I, my mother and dad had five daughters by then, would be at home across the street from two ladies who sat on their porch and watched out for us over across the street. And if we opened the door, she would say, okay, girls, or they would say, collectively sometimes, you know your mother does not want that door open after dark. Because that's what we did. That's what they did. All of the mothers looked after all of the children and there was no discussion. You were not going to say, miss So-and-so told me, so-and-so, you were not going to do that because all of the parents had the right to discipline.

My mom was Lucille Washington, and my dad was Levi Washington. My mother's name was Thompson. Her parents were Daniel Thompson and Effie Thompson. My father's side of the family we're just learning more about now. We didn't know a lot. My dad was the 13th child and basically raised himself on his own from the time he was about 13 years old. He started working in a garage in Trenton, learning to be a mechanic, and he became the best one there. I remember my mom said they would wake my dad up in the middle of the night to take him somewhere to fix a car, because he was really, really that good.

He did that a long time, but I don't know his (mother's names) I'm not sure. I don't want to call her name because I'm not quite sure what it was. My oldest sister was named for my grandmother, Effie, and my mother, Effie Lucile Washington McClellan was her maiden name.

And then I'm the next - Vivien Leigh Washington Filer. Then my (I always call her my baby sister) because she was a baby for ten years. There are two other sisters under her - she never gave up the babyhood. Sarah Frances Washington Brown and under Sarah is Karen, Karen Sue Washington Johnson. And then the baby girl is Cynthia Valencia Washington Powell.

The Cotton Club, Sarah's, Blue Note

I love talking about the Cotton Club - at that time and now the Cotton Club Museum, because a little-known history in Gainesville is about what Black folk did, who we were, where we were, what we established, and how we established it.

And I said this at one of the commission meetings because the mayor has me speak there once a month. And I said before I started to speak, that I was gonna highlight some African-American educators because it really appalled me, and I had to stop to wonder how prominent African-Americans could be in Gainesville and yet White Americans didn't even know they exist.

I said, I think that's privilege. I said, Mr. Mayor, you didn't invite me here for this - but I think it's very privileged for them (White people) to think that they don't need to know who we are. The Cotton Club Museum, and I say that because the lady who established the Cotton Club was an African-American entrepreneur in business way before her time, in Jim Crow, segregation. And she actually had a business downtown. That street at 1st Avenue, now that's closed off, was Union Street. Miss Sarah had a sandwich shop down there. Miss Sarah McKnight. And over across town on what was then Seminary Lane, which is now 5th Avenue, she had Sarah's place, Sarah's. I think that's what it was called.

But anyway, it was a trailer, like a diner sort of place that she sold food out of. And people came to play music - jam they called it- because she loved music. African-American musicians, along with University of Florida musicians, met there. They have since made a documentary on that.

Miss Sarah wanted a place where African-Americans could enjoy band music, big band, because big bands played, we know they played in white venues. White people dance and enjoy them. But there were no large places that Black bands could play for their own people. Hence, the Chitlin Circuit. The Chitlin Circuit existed in areas where there was a black hotel, and as you know, Gainesville had a black hotel, the Dunbar Hotel, not far from you in your neighborhood.

That building still exists. I tell everybody it's a two-story pink building behind the police station. We still are trying to get a marker there. But because that building existed, Gainesville became a member of the Chitlin Circuit. We learned all of this, and we started renovating that place, the Cotton Club, then my church purchased that 1.8 acres of land, and the building was sitting there.

And my minister said, "Sister Filer, I want you to see about saving that building." That was a very big challenge for me at the time, because that was not in my informational model at that time. Anyway, we did establish a board of directors and move on to make that into a museum, but the club existed because Miss Sarah opened it up and set it up so that big bands could come. So in through our doors and on the same stage that we have now came James Brown, B.B. King, Bo Diddley, Ella Fitzgerald, and B.B. King. You know, he's the big, big deal. So, it went for maybe a couple of years in fine shape. But soon as the commissioners or whoever was giving out the license in Gainesville learned that White kids from the university were coming over to dance and have fun at the museum, at the Cotton Club, they would not renew Miss Sarah's liquor license, and therefore the club had to close. But opened again as the Blue Note Club, which is why our doors are blue.

When it closed as The Blue Note, then it became a warehouse. But our local bands, I tell everybody we were so privileged and didn't know it. At our after-football dances, which were on 5th Avenue at the Wabash Hall there, that old red brick building, upstairs we would go to dance after football games. The football guys would go to school and shower and get dressed and come on up there and the rest of us would be waiting for the football team to get there.

But we had a live band playing every time. It was just great! One of the biggest was called Fat Papa's Band. This guy was talented. And I met his son lately and didn't get into his drumming, but he was a good singer, drummer, everything. And then Wilton Hendrix, those names came up. Wilton died not long ago, but there were quite a few. I don't remember a lot of them. There were quite a few great musicians who came through here. Miss McClellan, her husband, Field McClellan, and his brother Marion and those. They had a band. That band also played at the, at the Cotton Club when it was in existence as well. There's somebody else, probably, who knows a lot more about them, but those were some of the ones who brought music to Gainesville.

Dancing and Partying

Did I like to dance? Oh, I was the best. When I was in the ninth grade, I never liked the guys in ninth grade. They were just so immature. But I was a good dancer, and so was my friend. I have a classmate now - I won't call his name, but we brought him to our yard in the sand out there and taught him to dance. And then he taught the others. But me - jitterbug - that was my specialty.

And I remember in the, I don't know what grade, either 9th or 10th grade. My mother had said I couldn't go to this dance at the recreation center, which was the building that's now the Rosa Williams building. That's where we danced. But I was not allowed to go there on Tuesday night. That was a weekend kind of thing. I knew it was a dance contest. Some women's group, Black women's group, was having this contest and we were invited to come. So, I told my mother that I had to go to the library. Now, the building next to the Rosa Williams, was a library. They made that a library to keep Black kids from going downtown to the library. So that was our first library for Blacks there. So, I told my mom I had to go to the library, and I left my books at the library, but I went next door to the center.

And then Mrs. Dunbar's grandson, her son or grandson, he was a little short guy, but he was sharp on his feet. I mean, he was really good. And so, I only danced with him. We, of course, did the jitterbug. I was sweating all over, but we won first place. And then we didn't have newspaper coverage, except for a little column once a week, that they called, The Colored News. Then out comes this paper next week with me holding my 25-cent pack of notebook paper that I won at this dance, which I wasn't supposed to be at. Well, I was in trouble for a long time, but I remember that till today. That's been many years ago.

Final thoughts: *One of the things that was a problem for me growing up was that no one ever told me the historical significance of our neighborhoods. Pleasant Street, Seminary Lane, 5th Avenue, Porters Quarters, Sugarhill, and Springhill were always presented as other ghetto communities, places we wanted to hurry up and leave, and vow never to return to. No one ever mentioned the rich and significant impact that was birthed in our communities. I didn't learn about the value of Pleasant Street or the existence of the Cotton Club until I was in my late thirties!*

I contend that is the critically damaging disconnect. Our children have no clue about how important and fabulous we are. Mrs. Filer's (and the other elders') stories are one of the elements missing from our collective narrative. These stories allow us to see and celebrate our history with the history makers.

Stories such as Mrs. Filer's can help instill a level of pride in our children because hearing the stories from the actual person, in my opinion, makes that accomplishment more realistic and more accessible than reading about it in a book. Their stories may be used to renew a sense of community pride. Perhaps if they knew the significance and the importance of our neighborhoods, they would not only embrace it, but they would strive to imitate it and create a legacy of their own. Maybe if they knew that Mrs. Filer, Miss Rosa, and others are still alive right around the corner, they could come back and see their living history.

Midnight in the Swamp

One night after playing a wicked set
Bo Diddley took a walk in the woods
He had played really hard and rocked the house
No doubt he was feeling good

He noted how the humidity
Suddenly turned into a fine mist
He noticed how bright the moon shined
Making the stars seem to glisten and twist

He realized he had come to a marsh
That seemed to appear from nowhere
He was shocked to see a gator with a back full of eyes
Swimming and playing there

Then a sweet fragrance overtook him
And the marsh turned into a lake
And in the moon light
He beheld with delight
A Mersistah who began to awake

First he saw a puff of white smoke
Then a crown of nappy red hair
Then a tiny waist and a big FL booty
That seemed to be floating on air

"I am the Mother of all waters
And all that provides life to the world"
Bo said, "I thought you was special.
You don't look like no average girl"

"I hear you are a blues man
Whose music is wicked and sweet
If you have time
And you don't mind
Would you play a tune for me"

Now Bo wasn't one to deny a request
So, he tilted his hat and smiled
With one sensuous stroke
On that guitar axe
The swamp seemed to awake and go wild

He serenaded that Mersistah
Stirring passion and fire that night
And The Mother danced and giggled
Wiggling wickedly, popping her hips in delight

The stars, and planets and asteroids
Just had to get in on the show
They sparkled much brighter and heated up hot
Making the earth's crust burn hot down below

The fish, night birds and all God's creatures
Ran and pranced in a manner never seen
And Bo Diddley kept playing that fire
Even faster than in his wildest dreams

Then the sound of blue birds began to ring
Signaling the start of a brand new day
The Mother looked up high
And saw the Sun standing by
Marking the end of her night of play

Reluctantly she lifted her finger to her lips
And silenced her night family
She floated over to Bo and their gator friend
"Thanks Daddy for playing for me"

Just as she bent to give them a kiss
The sun raised up high and beamed bright
Bo woke up with a start
and a rapidly beating heart
Thinking this musta been one helluva night

Visions of that Mersistah
Danced and flickered in his head
He couldn't workout the pictures he saw
Til he noticed a new tat that said
The Mother was here!

He smiled and touched that tat
And through the swamp he made his way
Laughing to himself and humming a tune
About the awesome night and this beautiful new day

DUVAL HEIGHTS

Duval Heights has a long-standing history of excellence, with deep-rooted family and community ties. Originally established in the mid-20th century, Duval Heights grew as an African American neighborhood, home to families who were instrumental in building Gainesville's infrastructure and education system while boosting the local economy. Many residents worked and attended school at the University of Florida and Santa Fe, adding to Gainesville's highly educated and professional African American workforce. The community is also rich in entrepreneurial spirit and used to house many Black-owned businesses.

Over the years, Duval Heights has faced challenges related to housing instability and systemic neglect, typical of many of Gainesville's historically Black neighborhoods. In recent years, however, efforts have been made to address some of these long-standing issues through community initiatives, such as the Greater Duval Neighborhood Association. The Association, residents, and activists have worked to promote affordable housing, improve neighborhood safety, and provide educational and employment resources for the area's youth.

Duval Heights is undergoing further improvements as Gainesville invests in its East Side, which includes Duval Heights. New infrastructure projects, beautification efforts like the mural on the newly renovated Clarence R. Kelly Center, and community programs are underway to enhance residents' quality of life while preserving the neighborhood's unique history and character. Rest assured, community advocates closely monitor these interventions to ensure that gentrification and rising property costs do not displace long-time residents, striving to strike a balance between progress and preservation.

Yvette Clark: From Crosstown to Duval

I grew up on northeast 2nd Street in Gainesville. It's about two blocks east of Main Street, right near the old MacDuff store and the Goodyear Tire place. We had that whole little area there, by the little colored houses owned by Mr. Copes. And that's where we played and fought and raced and just had fun, you know, my friends, and sisters, brothers, and me.

It was seven of us, two of them are deceased. And so, there's five of us left but only two of us are still in Florida. So we're connected and keeping the traditions.

We lost my mom, Alice Buehler Robinson Stevens in 2023. We were one big family in the neighborhood. Every family knew everybody, we acknowledged our elders, and we obeyed them, because we didn't want to get, like, second whoopings.

We used to play games. Our favorite thing to do was have foot races. We would be racing up and down the street leading out to 16th Avenue and then over near the duck pond area. So that was our little haven, and we played marbles, we did jump rope, and jackstones. You know, we could go outside in the yard and play and be creative and do our own thing. We just had to be back in before the lights went on.

We'd come out at night and not be fighting with each other but having fun. We still had that competitive spirit among us. So, we had fights and stuff like that.

We had our own little personal games and competitions. We would also wait for the spray man to come down the street and spray that spray. We would run behind him, and that's probably why we can't think straight now. Those are some of the things that we did that brought a lot of joy to us.

One of the things I used to like to do was go out in the yard and play under this tree that had these pretty flowers, and that's where I would be, you know, making dirt pies or playing with the dirt. We used to go to McDuff appliance store and get the boxes that they would have the appliances in, and we would have races in the box out in the open field. I think it's a parking lot now for Goodyear.

We left Crosstown when I was about 5 or 6, and we moved farther east to the Duval area. I went to Duval Elementary School. When I was on 2nd Street, I went to A Quinn Jones and Sidney Lanier before it became a school for special needs kids. When we moved, Duval was my elementary school, then Howard Bishop, and Gainesville High.

We also went to Gainesville High School because that's when they closed Lincoln High School. A whole lot of stuff was going on at that time that was pretty scary. We were young kids, and we didn't really know about segregation and integration. We were just trying to stay out of trouble with Mama and Daddy. Once things settled down, we were able to go to high school and graduate successfully and figure out what we were going to do with the rest of our lives.

Sharnda Mosley – The Baby of the Bunch

I'm Sharnda Mosley, daughter of Wayne and Susie Mosley. Granddaughter of Lonnie and Carry Session as well as Lewis and Carry Mosley. I grew up in Duval Heights in Gainesville, FL. For me, one of my favorite childhood memories would be being able to just be outside after school. My grandmother was our after-school caretaker. She had a set schedule for us. When we came home, she had a meal cooked, which she used to call supper. We would eat, do our homework and by 4:30, 5 o'clock we were out the door. You had to be back inside the house by the time the streetlights came on and you stayed in the neighborhood. You know being able to socialize with the people I grew up with in the neighborhood. Going in and out of my neighbors' doors. Being down in Gardenia (apartments) playing kickball. Playing in makeup. Different stuff like that. Being able to safely socialize with others my age.

One thing that sticks out for me is Sunday night at Skate Station and being able to go with my brother. Me and my brother are nine years apart, so he always had to take me along wherever he went. I remember the New Edition concert there. I remember when Boys to Men came there. It was one of those places that stuck out. It's still standing, but it doesn't have the same significance. Like for Soulful Sundays back in the day. We went out; but it was over at ten o'clock.

Terri: How do you feel about the gentrification that's happening in Black neighborhoods?

Sharnda: I believe we're at a disadvantage in two ways, economically and socially. Most of the generation behind us, my children's generation and below, don't know the value of heritage, and they can't appreciate the Black community or the Black neighborhood. I also feel that we're taken advantage of a lot.

Terri: What do you feel is one thing that kids don't get growing up in a Black, closeknit neighborhood like you did?

Sharnda: I may be an exception to that question for the mere fact that when my kids were young - my kids are now almost 30 - the older population, my grandmother, and Miss Jenkins across the street, they were still vibrant. My grandmother walked to the end of the street every day to watch my daughter walk home from Duval Elementary, which is the same thing she did for me. So, my kids got a taste of it. My grandmother, who unfortunately has gone on, was 98 when she passed away. She lived a very long life, and she was still able to be our hero and install in my kids and my brother's kids things that she did for us. Now my grandkids, on the other hand, are a whole different story.

Carlos Nelson – My Childhood Meant Freedom Sharnda and Carlos

My name is Carlos Nelson. I was born at Alachua General Hospital in 1967 in Gainesville, FL. We started out in Fairbanks and then we moved down to Lake Road, where we lived for a good 20-something years, all of my youth. Then we moved over here to 928, in Duval.

Terri: What is your favorite childhood memory about growing up in a Black neighborhood?

Carlos: As a young Black guy, I was able to walk the streets freely from this house to my mom's beauty shop every day, with no supervision, to do work and come back home. That was one of my biggest memories. Not having to worry about people (bothering you) and different things that's going on.

Terri: What do you think younger kids now are missing that we had growing up?

Carlos: They are missing grandparents. It is nothing like the older generation which you don't have now. These younger grandmas aren't cutting it. I think kids are missing the older generations and things being passed down. Being with grandma, getting things done in the kitchen, learning something to be passed down.

Patricia J. Powers – A Californian in Duval Heights

My name is Patricia J. Powers. My mother was Emonia Savoy, of San Francisco, California. I married Willie F. Powers and came here in 1961. We lived with my mother-in-law, Willivera Dixon, on 22nd Street and 8th Avenue. The Dixons, and The Mitchells, were the first people on that street. There was no apartment, no homes, no nothing. I lived there for a while.

Life in Duval, coming from a big city like San Francisco, was hard. When we came to Gainesville, we came on the train. We were on the train all the way through. When we got to Jacksonville, they put us in the caboose. And you had to go into the kitchen without Whites and, warm up my baby milk. I walked in that kitchen and there were roaches everywhere. I said, "no, no, no." She would starve all the way to Gainesville. I would not do it.

In Gainesville, you had just two houses you could look at, you know, and outside bathrooms. It was pretty hard, but I lived with it. Then finally, my husband's grandmother bought us a home on 25th Street. We became the third couple. There still was no other houses up there, no apartment or anything. That was in '62, so we had indoor plumbing.

And we were back in the woods. I remember my mother-in-law used to walk me down the street and behind 8th Avenue, all the way in the back. There was like a church, well, the church. And she used to show me where Black people were lynched back up in there.

And I saw all that in the trees. They still had the rope hanging. And I remember crying and calling my mother in California and telling her about, you know, what you go through, in the South. When I had children, I kept my kids close by me. And every morning, we would sit on the porch (because they weren't ready for school) and let them see what was going on, the birds and all that different stuff. It wasn't a bad life, but it was a different life, you know, that I never had seen before.

I taught them to be kind to everybody, you know, because I was used to being integrated and it wasn't like that in the South. So, I had to teach them that. I told them, "Remember, you are very important and always feel that way." Tanya Jorner, Willie L. Powers, and Aleida Scott. My greatest thing, I think, is my children. And I thank God for them every day.

We were happy when others started moving where we were, because we had people we could talk to and see every morning. Instead of just sitting on the porch and combing my two girls' hair. I didn't have nothing to look at, but now I got neighbors I can talk to.

My girls went to school at Gainesville High School, because I worked at the University of Florida and then Willie, he decided he wanted to go to PK Young. And so, we decided, okay, we'll let him go. And then he got into basketball. Then he got into football, but he got hurt in football. Somebody knocked him down. And I went on the field crying, "No football, no more!"
That was my only son. Then Willie decided, "Oh, I'm going to go to Florida A&M University. Mama, I'm going to be big." He went there and played basketball. He had to cry to come home. But he went back to college and graduated from it.

While the kids went to school I worked for the guy who invented Gatorade, Dr. Cade. I worked in the Department of Medicine. I was a phlebotomist. I draw blood and take care of kidney patients. And then I got up an organization called HELP for kidney patients; I ran a bingo (game night) for about 40 years to raise money to keep them (patients) going. And Dr. Cade was always there to furnish the money and make sure everything was okay. HELP stood for Help Each of us Live Prosperously.

My husband has been dead for three years. The Duncan's and them helped to get his name put on 25th Street. So that has been joyful for me, knowing that at least he got to see before he died.

I think of what my mother said to me, "You made it, you stay there, and you take care of it." Because I wanted to go home. She said, "No, you wanted that husband, you stay there."

And I'm from a Catholic family. And that's what my family believed in. My inheritance is my grandmother was Irish. My dad was French. And my momma had some Mexican, that's what it said in her blood. My husband used to say, "Yeah, that's why you're a fighter."

Willie was a phlebotomist. He worked at the VA for almost 40 years. And he was the first Black slow pitch baseball hitter. He integrated Starke. He hit the ball so far! And we were in Starke one night and my husband had beat the team so badly with home runs that they had to come and get us because the Klansmen was coming. WW Gay and them, took us all the way home by the back roads, to get us back in Gainesville.

My children have had some experiences. And it's a good thing because now they know. But I teach my children, you know, in your family in California, you don't know who or what they are half the time! You don't know if they Black, Yellow, or White. Just treat everybody like you want to be treated. And that's what I think my kids do.

I would like to see a little more love for kids today, a little more where parents take more time with them, do things with them. And if they do something wrong and don't own it, make sure they do the right thing. That's how I have always been. A long time ago, if somebody come from next door and they said you did something wrong, you're gonna get a beating.

They believed in that. I try to make my kids be the same way. And sometimes they still got with the wrong kids. My grandson, he plays for Hawthorne, and I tell him, "You don't do what everybody else do." You know that vapor (vaping) and all that different stuff the kids got now, I try to put in his head, "it's not good for you."

I try to make sure that they do the right thing. I can't make them do it, but I try to help them.

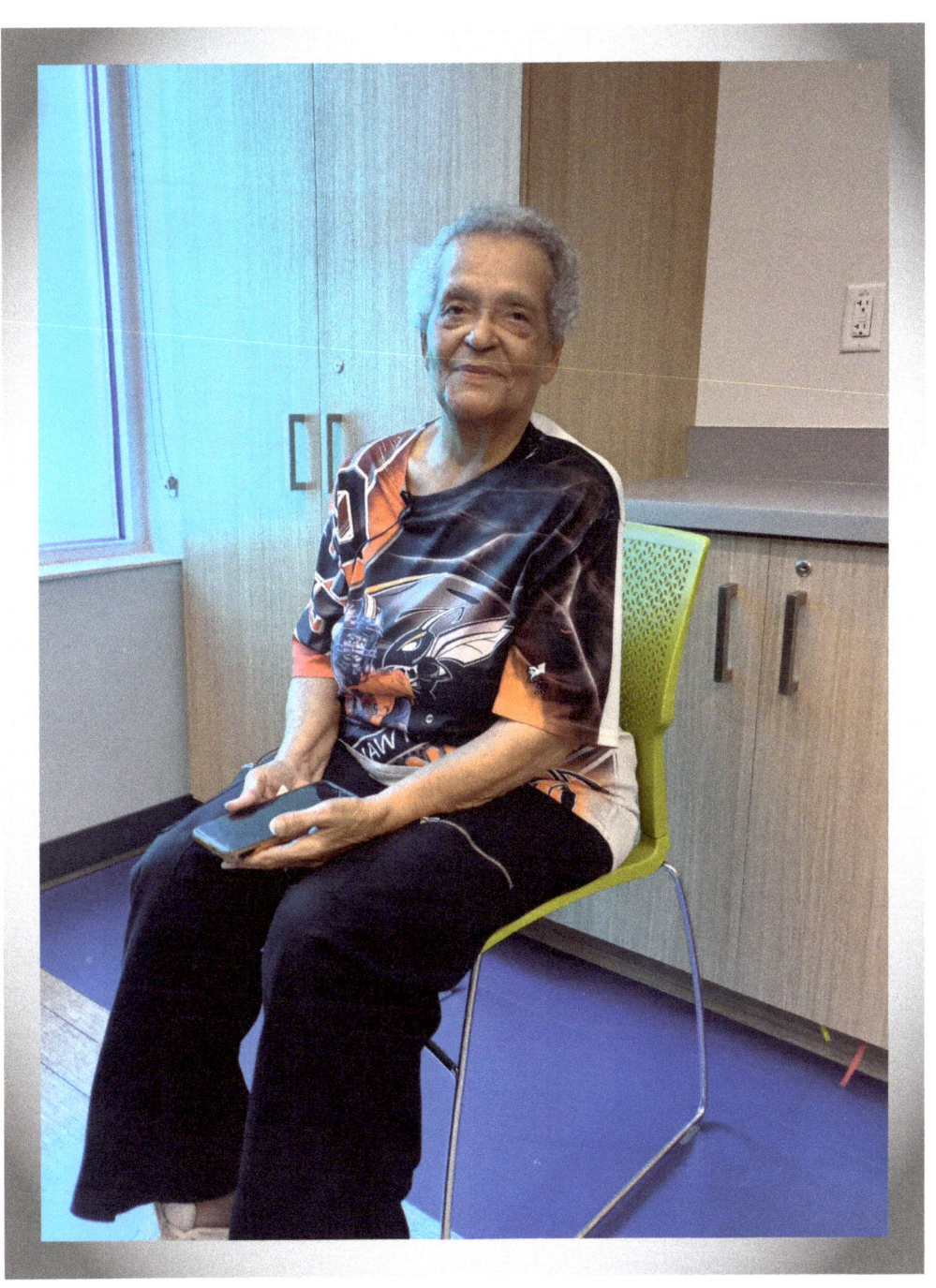

CARVER GARDENS

Carver Gardens Apartments, located in SE Gainesville, is a residential community established in 1970. The complex comprises 100 units spread across two stories, offering one, two, and three-bedroom apartments. As a HUD-subsidized property, Carver Gardens provides affordable housing options.

Carver Gardens is located a few miles from the University of Florida, which makes it conveniently accessible for its students and dangerously on the path of development. Its sister housing project, Kennedy Homes, was demolished with promises to rebuild that were never honored. This left a noticeable hole in Gainesville's affordable housing offerings.

Fortunately, the Gainesville Housing Authority has retained Carver Gardens as an essential part of its commitment to providing affordable housing within the Gainesville area. This commitment is crucial to contributing to the city's diverse residential landscape, ensuring that everyone, regardless of their income, has a place to call home.

Robert Jammer: Bikes, Basketball, and Lessons from the Big Boys in Carver Gardens

I'm Robert Jammer, and my parents are Roslyn and Robert Jammer. I'm representing the Carver Gardens Apartments on SE 15th St. in Gainesville, FL. Growing up in Carver Gardens was good. I was very young when I lived there. I think we moved away when I was eleven. So, from zero to eleven, that's where I lived. It was great! We lived in apartment 87, which was upstairs in the back kind of, after a couple of speed humps. It was always fun. We had neighbors that would always come up and look for me and my brothers. I had two younger brothers. We were kind of the neighborhood boys to come and hang out and play with. We were athletic, and we used to all ride bikes together. We used to be out there 30 deep with our bikes, skates, and rollerblades. You know, it was that era.

Basketball, for sure, was my favorite childhood game. It was the challenge of playing with bigger boys, you know. There were a lot of older guys in the neighborhood, and so I used to always wanna play with them. I never wanted to play with guys that was my age or my size. I was always interested in playing with the big boys, and they wanted me to play too. Kids don't have that outdoor neighborhood thing anymore. It was a kind of mentoring. You saw them (the older boys) starting out riding their bikes and walking around, and then they got older and now they got girlfriends, and you got to see everything happening, you know, right in front of you. It was an evolution. So yes, that is a part that's missing because people aren't really as open, don't come outside as much (and people aren't), showing as much life as they used to.

Carver Gardens is in the Lincoln Estate neighborhood, so I used to walk around to Miss Tate house and get the squeeze cups. You know, I have that whole experience of being able to know the candy lady and trying to swipe what I can! Yeah, it was just a different time. Growing up in Carver Gardens they didn't cut the fire hydrants on, but they had water, you know jump around through there and have a good time.

We definitely had a few bad apples, like crackheads, drug users, out there! They used to ride around on their bikes and sing their songs. It was Sam and them! We definitely had some local, you know, celebrity crackheads for sure. They were legendary! We were right next to Kennedy Homes too, so we used to go over there all the time. We were familiar with the local crack problems. Now gentrification is something that is alarming; that needs to be talked about for sure. It's not fair that they have set up these situations where they're pushing the Black people out of our neighborhoods and displacing us. They're not allowing us to have our history, homes, and land that we had for centuries you know. It is an ugly thing for sure.

LAKE ROAD

Lake Road Apartments in Gainesville, Florida, is an enduring residential community originally developed as affordable housing for low—and moderate-income families. Like many HUD-funded properties from past decades, the complex has faced challenges, including maintenance issues and aging infrastructure. Over the years, there has been a growing need to revitalize the property to provide residents with safe, modern housing.

In 2023, HUD allocated funding for the renovation of Lake Road Apartments as part of an initiative to update affordable housing units across the nation. According to the March 2024 article, Gainesville Housing Authority to update residents on Status of HUD grant, by Gainesville Sun reporter Voleer Thomas, "The housing authority and the city of Gainesville were awarded a $500,000 Choice Neighborhoods Planning Grant from the federal government to create a plan to redevelop GHA's Lake Terrace and Pine Meadows properties and improve the surrounding East University Avenue neighborhood. The Choice Neighborhood includes Duval Heights and North Lincoln Heights."

This renovation plan is designed to improve building structures, update utilities and energy systems, and enhance amenities to ensure compliance with safety and accessibility standards. The project is expected to include new plumbing, electrical updates, and potentially even eco-friendly upgrades to reduce environmental impact and operational costs. These improvements will enhance current residents' quality of life and support HUD's mission to provide sustainable, affordable housing in communities like Gainesville.

The HUD grant also funds the Gainesville Housing Authority's Community Ambassador Program. Dominique Pinder and Tabatha Williams are both Ambassadors from Lake Road/Lake Terrace/Pine Meadows neighborhoods.

Tabitha Williams and The Easter Hairstyle

My name is Tabitha Williams. My maiden name is Austin. My mother's name is Sheila Foxworth Christie. My daddy's name is Herbert Austin, and they're from Sugar Hill Robinson Quarters.

Robinson Quarters is across the street from Woodland Park. My grandparents let me know that it was the original Sugar Hill. Robinson Quarters was a small apartment complex. My grandfather, Bill Scott, and Mr. Robinson built those apartments before they remodeled them. My great grandmother is Mary Scott.

Growing up there was fun. It was all about the community. It was all about love; and the networking was awesome because they all got along, and they all supported one another. When they say it takes a village to raise a child, everybody pitched in and helped each other's household. My grandmother always cooked a large dinner, and she invited the neighborhood. The majority of her friends pretty much did the same thing.

We were a very tight network. I love that because that's how we got to know everybody. Like Miss Mildred Dewberry, she stayed in Robinson Quarters as well, she played the piano. She's my uncle's grandmother. She and my grandmother, Bernice Foxworth were close friends. So just having that strong network, that strong community, that's what I liked.

Now I stay in Pine Meadows on Lake Road, under Gainesville Housing Authority. I am a Community Ambassador. The reason that I took the role as a Community Ambassador was because I really wanted to be that person speaking up for my community, and to let my community know that there is hope. There is hope for change, but we have to be determined and we're gonna have to come together. God always let me know that a threefold cord is not easily broken. So, when we come together, we form a real tight net that's not easy to break.

One thing I didn't like growing up was my grandma doing my hair with the original straightening comb for Easter. I would cry and cry because I had this long hair. We didn't go to church too much, but back then my grandmother was going to Williams Temple. I knew that Easter was coming when I'd see her pulling out those curling irons and that hot comb. I would know when I saw those things, we were gonna go through it with that Blue Magic hair grease.

Dominique Pinder — Community Events Remind Me of Home

My name is Dominique Pinder, and I represent the Lake Terrace neighborhood. I'm originally from Freeport, Grand Bahama, the Bahamas. We refer to Lake Terrace as Lake Road as well. I've been living here about five years. I'm a single mom, and I'm raising my four kids (aged nine up to 15) here.

One thing I kind of cherish is being able to go to the park and play with my kids, have picnics, and you know have one-on-one time. My youngest, in particular, looks forward to going to Fred Cone Park. He and I play sports, and he wants to be an athlete when he gets older. My other kids just go out there for fun.

It's kind of a close-knit community. We have events and stuff that I would say is similar to home (in the Bahamas). Like Juneteenth, my kids look forward to that every year. That's one thing that's similar. We need more development for our youth. We need things to keep them less distracted, especially our young boys. You know, things that would keep them off the streets. I feel like they could be learning trades. We can bring our community together by finding people that are educated or experienced in those fields, and they can also like mentor- not only to the boys, but all our youth.

Marriette Ellis – My Family Friendly Neighborhood

My name is Marriette Ellis, and I'm representing Lake Road here in Gainesville, FL. My mother's name is Vivian Ellis, my father's name is Morris Ellis, my sibling's names are Fontella Ellis, and my sister, who just passed a year ago, Lakenya Ellis,

Growing up, Lake Road was always such a family-friendly/oriented environment. I really loved it. I think as I've grown up I've learned to appreciate the environment that I grew up in. You know you never really know how much of an effect the place, or you know the people, has on you until you grow up and you look back. So, it was an amazing, amazing starting point for me. I'm very family-friendly, so I loved being raised there.

One of my fondest memories was playing with friends. I know that we have to be careful now - we had to be careful back then too, but it just seems like it's so much (more) stuff that's going on right now. But one of my fondest memories at that time was being able to be outside with friends and family, playing, riding our bikes, walking to the store in a group. Yes, so that was one of my fondest memories.

LINCOLN ESTATES

Lincoln Estates, built between 1960 and 1978, is a place of historical significance, containing approximately 600 homes. The community was nationally recognized as a model that brought equitable access to homeownership to Black Americans. In Gainesville, Lincoln Estates became home to the Black elite, offering upscale housing, school access, and a strong sense of community. Lincoln Estates symbolizes perseverance and demonstrates the ability of Black families to thrive despite the systemic challenges of racism, redlining, and limited access to economic opportunities.

As time passed, the community saw generational growth, with homes passed down to children and grandchildren, strengthening the cultural and familial bonds that defined the area. Lincoln Estates became known for its deep roots, with residents maintaining a solid commitment to preserving their neighborhood's character. However, in recent years, Lincoln Estates has faced increasing pressure from gentrification, which ushers in an influx of White occupants and reshapes the neighborhood's character and culture. Because of gentrification, some long-time residents may need help to remain members of the community due to rising taxes and housing costs.

As with other historically predominantly Black communities, Lincoln Estates' location near the University of Florida, Santa Fe College Downtown Campus, and downtown Gainesville has made it attractive to developers wishing to capitalize on its proximity to the city's student population. The residents of Lincoln Estates stand at a crossroads, fighting to protect their homes and preserve their legacy.

Students protesting the closure of the predominantly black Lincoln High School as part of Alachua County integrating the public school system.

From the Florida Photograph Collection, George A. Smathers Libraries, University of Florida.

Delvon Filer: Continuing a Family Legacy of Service

I am Delvon Filer. I am 24 years old and studying biotechnology. My father is Delano Filer, son of Robert Filer and Essiemae Filer. My mother is Calpurnia Crawford, daughter of Mary Crawford. Not sure who her father is, unfortunately. In my family there are a couple of famous people from around Gainesville. My aunt, Vivian Filler, is one of them and Delano Filler, who I believe worked at Hawthorne High School.

My neighborhood was pretty quiet. I stayed around Lincoln Estates pretty much. Most of my days were spent there at my grandma's house. Growing up, people kinda looked out for you. Like if you wanted something from the corner store or something, people would just give you a li'l bit of money. Like you're walking down the street, and someone would be like "Hey! You want a few dollars for some candy or something like that?"

I try to help out and be that person for younger kids when I can.

Mr. Sam B Wesley the Second, of Katie Heights, Chronicles the Power of Owning Businesses in Black Communities

I grew up in what was called Katie Heights now North Lincoln Heights. I got a whole bunch of memories, yeah. You want me to name 'em all?

I remember the little stores that was owned by African Americans. Like it was a launderette in my neighborhood. I remember Mr. Strawder had a little store. I remember Mr. Clark Butler used to come in our neighborhood and collect rent.

I was looking at those people because I knew I wanted to own my own business. I remember when segregation first started, and they closed down Lincoln High School and when they open Eastside - I went to Eastside and graduated from Eastside. I also went to Buchholz for a short period of time, but I have many memories of growing up in Gainesville.

When it comes to what they doing to our communities now, on one hand I think it's good based on the areas that you're talking about. In the areas that are drug infested; change has gotta come - it's inevitable. In the areas where you got historical businesses and people who are paying their taxes and they're doing something like eminent domain, which I'm not aware of they're doing, I wouldn't be for that. But the free market kind of dictates where people's gonna build and if we are responsible and pay our taxes and protect our land, which I think is the utmost important, then once we get it we keep it and not sell it, but my feelings is mixed on that subject.

I had some businesses in Pleasant Street, Crosstown. Like my laundromat, which is the old Glasper Cleaners in my neighborhood that I used to go to when I was a little kid. Well, they used to wash the Lincoln High School band uniforms, and it was the oldest laundromat and dry cleaners in the city of Gainesville. It was Airway Cleaners, well now it is Airway Cleaners by Sam B Wesley the Second. Here on 5th Avenue, the building used to have Roosevelt Branch and people would come out (to go to his place). I don't even remember all (the places from) when I was a kid. I came over here myself, but this house/this building housed many African American businesses over the period of time. And it was kind of like the center where you could find multiple African American owned businesses in one building. Today, we still carry on that tradition as we got my bail bonds, we got Jared Gaines, who fixes computers, you got Michael Perkins, who does income taxes and who's an accountant, and things of that nature. But, at any rate, this building has been a staple of this neighborhood for years. It has always been a necessity to have commercial property in our neighborhood where we can work and play just like they do in Haile Plantation.

I remember those days. I went to Friendship Baptist Church around there - I used to sneak down there, to Reverend Cato. And Mr. Williams had a store on the corner down there, on the corner I think it's 3rd and 5th. I used to sneak out of church and come down here, spend my money and get back to church and get in trouble.

I'm from Gainesville. My family on my mother's side from Marion County, but my dad's side was in Gainesville, and I grew up much of my life traveling between the two. My mother's father fought in World War One and he's from Micanopy and they always honor him. His name was Ed Reese. On my father's side, most don't live in Gainesville now. When school was out I had to go to Marion County and go in the fields and pick whatever that season was. When school was in I had to come back and go to Williams elementary, Westwood, Eastside, Bucholz - I went to school. And I loved school. I used to hate to go to the fields, so I even went to summer school to make sure not to go in those fields.

Tanisha Byers: Good Old Time in Lincoln Estates

My name is Tanisha Byers. My mother is Juanita Thomas. She originates from Eutaw, Alabama. My father is Tyree Thompson, and he originates from New Haven, CT., and I grew up in Lincoln Estates. I have a lot of childhood memories from Lincoln Estates.

Well, things we liked to do when we were little…we would go through the woods and pick blackberries off the bushes. We would build clubhouses in the woods and have our little club meetings. We would try to sell stuff to make money for our little club. I don't know what we were going to do with the money. We rode our bikes. My grandmother lived in Spring Hill, so I was over there a lot. I rode my bike from Lincoln Estates to Spring Hill.

We just had a good ol' time! We explored the area. We walked up to T.B. McPhearson to go to the park. Walked to the candy lady for squeeze cups – all of the childhood things. I went to a couple of dances at T.B., but I went with the wrong people and got kicked out. I ain't have no business up in there anyway! My momma ain't know where I was. Kids today don't get to experience your neighbors looking out for you. I mean back then, they would tell on you, and they would snitch on you, but they were looking out for you. They were trying to keep you safe. If they see you doing something they ain't got no business (doing), they gonna call your momma. When you get home, your momma already knew what you have been up to. I wish I had that for my kids when they were growing up. Like if my kid was lost now, nobody would know where they were.

From Pistol Alley to Lincoln Estates, God is in Charge
Mary Perry Issacs

My name is Mary Perry Isaac. My dad's name is Emmett Perry, and my mom's name is Teretha Perry and I'm from Lincoln Estates. Lincoln Estates was good for me in 1962, and then I moved out of that neighborhood and moved on my own. I lived in Sugar Hill. Now I'm in Norwood Oaks, out by Eastside High School. And that's a predominantly Black neighborhood.

Terri: How long did you stay over in Sugar Hill?

Ms. Mary: About eight years. I was middle aged. I raised two boys over there in Sugar Hill, but we never did anything in Sugar Hill. I always took them out of the neighborhood. There were so many children out there raising themselves. And if they were raising themselves, they weren't the very best. I didn't wanna get in a confrontation with the parents or the children. I just took my kids out of the neighborhood.

Terri: I respect that. What type of things would y'all do when you would go out?

Ms. Mary: Well, I played basketball all through my years and my sons played basketball and softball, and so I used to do that. We used to go out of town to Disney World and everywhere there was water, like Daytona Beach. We did a lot of traveling because I had two sons, Alozi and Savondrick, and I was raising them basically by myself.

Eastwood is okay. I mean, you know, if you stay in your place and don't try to visit the other apartments and the, well, it's a house out there. You can do good if you just tend to your business and leave out of the neighborhood. I call that the country, then I come into the city and do what I need to do.

Terri: And so where did you grow up at?

Ms. Mary: We call it the Pistol Alley behind Chestnuts Funeral Home. Oh, it was so nice. Yup, it was like three or four families. They raised everybody. They could spank and discipline everybody's children. It was the Davis family back there. It was the Perry family back there. It was the Lindseys, the Roberts and the McCoys. I think that was their name. And everybody's children, we listened to everybody. And nobody better not tell Mr. Perry or Ms. Perry something they saw us do. We would beg them not to tell because we know what we would get.

Terri: What is one of your favorite childhood memories?

Ms. Mary: I had an identical twin sister. We looked just alike. Her name was Martha and my name was Mary. And we grew up together and we used to aggravate the schoolteachers because they didn't know us apart. My daddy really didn't know us apart, but he tied a red piece of yarn around my sister's wrist. But we used to fool our boyfriends, husbands, and our children.
You know because we looked so much alike, you know, and stuff like that. We just had a good time. We loved each other. We went everywhere together, done everything together. Even if we had to fight one person, the two of us would do it together. We just had the best time, you know, growing up.

We used to jump springboard. With two big tires in the middle, stacked up one on top of the other and a long board laying across it horizontally. And the board had to be wide. And we just pump each other up in the air. And you know, Charles Chestnut? We taught him how to jump springboard. He was a crybaby back in the day. Because he grew up with a nanny and grandparents. So, he was like uh, spoiled.

We grew up, we didn't fight. My mom and them didn't have to look out the window to see what we were doing out there. We knew we had to be home when the city lights, come on. It was a good life.

Terri: Not many people talk about Pistol Alley.

Ms. Mary: We used to have reunions over there, but once Miss Irene Davis, passed away, Templee Davis passed away, Ovala Lumpkin, she passed away (they stopped). But I think the last family reunion we had over there was maybe eight years ago. We wanna start back doing that again.

Terri: What do you feel is one thing missing from the Black community in Gainesville now?

Ms. Mary: If you don't have Jesus in your life, you don't have anything, So, you have to raise your children up that (Christian) way. Back in the day, I tried, I never drank, smoked, used drugs, or anything like that, never. And I could have, you know, I did a lot of things back in the day that wasn't right. But now I don't do that. I just try to live my life the best that I can, and I use the Bible for the way that I live. And the way I try to be and treat other people. I attend 10th Avenue Church of Christ; the minister is Adrian Hopper.

MULTIPLE NEIGHBORHOODS RESIDENTS

Alexandria Gibson: Celebrating a Bahamian Legacy in Historic Black Gainesville

My name is Alexandria Gibson; in the neighborhood, I go by Danielle. I am the daughter of Charlene Rigby and Alexander Gibson. I'm one of those 'hood babies who moved around a lot. We started out in Oak Ridge, it's a place a lot of people don't know about. It's one of those old projects nestled between 441 and 6th Street. Right after Gene, Jim, and Roy, where they sell mobile home trailers. When I was a kid, it looked so huge, but when I drive by now, it's got to be the smallest projects in town.

When we left the Bahamas and came here, we lived there first. These are my earliest memories in Oak Ridge, so I'm guessing my age was between three and five. In Oak Ridge, I have very fond memories of crab pot. That's when my mom was still young, and still cooked crabs all the time, with pig feet. I just remember seeing the pot. I remember my mom being the neighborhood *it* girl. There was always a lot of people around and parties.

I can still remember all my neighbors and the apartments we lived in. The lady to the left of us, her name was Cooly, and she was from Hawaii. I can never forget her. You know, we had the squeeze cup man who also did haircuts there. Then the girl upstairs was one of my babysitters. So, when I say my mom was the *it* girl, I knew everybody out there. My mom did nails, so by her being the nail lady in every neighborhood we lived in, she was always very popular.

We used to be able to just run the streets. When I think about that era, you know, I guess in hindsight, everybody was watching us, but nobody was watching us. When I think about the freedom and liberty I had in the hood at those ages. I think that's like the beautiful thing about the hood. You can go outside and play. Like in the suburbs, there's really nobody outside. But in the hood, everybody's outside. Everybody's doors are open; everybody's windows are up. That was before I had a bike, so we were on foot, just playing.

I remember when Michael Jackson's song, "Remember the Times" was out and Uncle Luke too. I don't know what we were doing listening to that music, but I remember in Oak Ridge, being on the concrete doing the crybaby, dry humping the ground. You know, us bad asses! My mom used to still dance back then. I'm the oldest child, so I have these fond memories of her in the hood that the other kids don't have.

From Oak Ridge, we moved to Pine Ridge. By the time we got to Pine Ridge, I was in kindergarten, I guess. Pine Ridge was a much bigger neighborhood, but we still used to be running the streets as little kids. There was a three-street block of Pine Ridge where we could run because all of our friends lived there. You just knock on the door and ask can so and so come outside and play. Before you knew it there would be like six or seven of us running around.

I was the first one that had a Nintendo. The old school Nintendo, the gray square one. So, everybody used to come to my house. All the boys used to come to my house so we could play Nintendo. We would be like dumpster diving; well not really diving, because we were too little to dive in the dumpster. But somehow we would get stuff out of the trash to play with. Once we got this Easy Bake Oven out of the garbage and plugged it up in the outside sockets! We would be taking toys out of the trash. I don't even know if my mom knows this stuff! It was insane.

When I was little, I didn't really understand the crack epidemic at that time, but I can definitely recall there were crackheads on bikes who used to sell Christmas trees, ornaments, and stuff.

But my fondest memories of Pine Ridge, and one of my first memories of church, came from Pine Ridge. A lady named Miss Flowers, I believe she still has a church in Ocala or somewhere. Miss Flowers used to ride around in her station wagon and pick up all the kids in the neighborhood, all the little five-year-olds, because she had a grandson that was our age. She would pick up all the kids she could fit in the car.

She would be like, "Can I take your baby to church?"

She would take us all the way in the country to this church. On the way to church, she would teach us a song and by the time we made it to church, we knew that song. I remember one time she taught us, "When the Saints Go Marching In" and when we got to church, she lined us up, and we had to sing the song, walk into the church, and put on a whole show. Yeah, my oldest church memories come from my Pine Ridge days, for sure.

In my teenage years, we lived in Village Green a little bit. It wasn't like it is now. Now they got all these gates, and they knocked down all the woods, and you can see right in Village Green. And all those gates make one way in and one way out. It was not like that when I was a kid. We had more freedom to move in and out. I think we lived in building G – G30. Village Green was a little different because I was older. I was a teenager, so I wasn't allowed to wander far, so I used to sit on the steps (I wasn't allowed to go further) and watch all the fights. It was a fight like every day. But it wasn't like it is now. The police weren't coming. Nobody was going to jail. Just friendly rumbles, I guess.

I used to run a babysitting business in Village Green. I would babysit your kids for ten dollars and, I didn't even know to put a time on it, you know, like an hour or two. My mama used to be so mad because I'd be gone for hours watching people's kids. She was like, "I'll give you ten dollars!"

Oh! You know, Village Green had the best candy lady out of them all because she used to put fruit – like pineapples - in the bottom of her freeze cups! It didn't matter if you got the red or whatever, it had some pineapple on the bottom. She was a real old lady. She had to be eighty-something back then.

Truthfully, now, you can't trust your kids outside as much when there are other races present. I hate to sound like integration was a bad thing, but when there were all Black people outside watching your kids or living in a Black neighborhood, you're more comfortable with your kids being outside.

CARLA LEWIS: A Powerful Advocate for Gainesville's Black Communities

Terri: I want to say thank you for all the great work that you do in multiple communities in Gainesville. You have made such a positive difference in our community. Tell me who you are, who you represent, what neighborhood, and talk a little bit about your lineage.

Carla: My name is Carla Lewis. I'm the project manager for SPARC 352, a community-based art program that is intended to empower artists and to give communities a way to use art as a tool for healing and for reckoning and for social change.
I am from a couple of different places. I was born here (Gainesville) at Shands Hospital, but not as a resident of Gainesville. We were from a little small town called Gordon Chapel.

I am a Baker from Gordon Chapel. One of the largest families anywhere in this area. So, it's Bakers, Gordons, Hutchesons, and Williams. Those are my combined family. My great-great-grandmother had 14 children. And then my great-grandmother had 11. My grandmother had nine. So, it stands to reason that we come from a pretty big family, right?

But from Hawthorne, the first place that we lived in the city of Gainesville with my parents was an apartment complex called Kennedy Homes. We grew up there. And when I say grew up there, our entire family moved to Gainesville like in 1971, 72. Mom got a job at an old store called GC Murphy, and my daddy was working at Florida Friers, which was a chicken plant that was here in the area. And that was considered money. They were doing okay.

And so, they moved from our trailer in Hawthorne into a four-bedroom apartment. But she moved her mom in. She moved her grandmother in. So, it was my mom, my dad, my grandmother, my great-grandmother, two of my uncles, two of my aunts, and myself and my brother. We all lived in a four-bedroom apartment in Kennedy Homes.

In 1974, my mom got a job at the phone company, which meant she was sure enough making some money back then. She said when she was hired, she made $95 a week, $400 a month. She was doing the thing. And so, she moved us to the Duval community where she still lives now. She's been in that house. But my grandmother and my great-grandmother both got apartments of their own in Kennedy Homes. So, I had a dual childhood because I spent most of the time with my grandparents because my mom was working. And so, I was in Kennedy Homes all day. And because my mom had five, six brothers and sisters, you know, we were kind of a big family, and my aunts were really popular. And my grandmother was really popular in the complex as well. That was just my mother's side. Now, a little bit of my dad's side. My father's father is from a place called Clarendon in the West Indies in Jamaica. When people ask me about my Jamaican heritage, I acknowledge it always. But what's at my core is being African in America. My paternal great grandfather was Daniel Lewis. I don't have a record of his family before then. But he's Daniel Lewis. On my dad's mother's side, my great-great-grandmother was Mary Baker (Williams). And my grandmother was Bertha Baker. My great-grandmother was Bertha Baker. My grandmother was Rosetta Baker.

My mom's side is the family that I grew up with the most. When my grandmother died, my great-great-grandmother's Bible was passed down to us. Someone had given it to her in 1932. It lists in there her parents as freed slaves from Alabama. And lists them as Sarah and McKinley Moore. And so, I take them as mine. Her name was Maggie Moore Brown. She had recorded in there every birth, wedding, everything. And when she died in 1957, (my grandmother's name was Ethel May), my great-grandmother continued the tradition. So, you can see the handwriting change from here to there. And the last thing that she recorded was the birth of one of my cousins. One of the first things that she recorded was my parents' birth. My great-great-grandmother recorded my mother's birth. You know what I mean? So just seeing that in there. And then you see an inscription from my grandmother when she was six years old. Her six-year-old self, wrote in the back, "This is my grandma's Bible. Nobody touch it." And everybody's like, "That's Eartha." It's definitely her. Her name was Eartha. My grandmother and my great-grandmother were like besties, like Thelma and Louise. Listen, they used to come and kidnap all the children and take care of us, while the parents worked. So, we spent most of our time with them.

Terri: That's beautiful, and such a blessing because most Black folk can't go that far back.

Carla: My great-grandmother, who I'm going to talk about in a few, her dad was 107 when he passed away. And I didn't even get to my mother's father's family, where there was also, longevity. I knew my great-great-grandmother Mary, who I could not stand, still wore prairie dresses and was a devout Christian. She was the meanest little thing, but she taught me how to clean chitlins (chitterlings/pork intestines). She taught me how to cook.

We was on a step stool in the kitchen, listening to gospel music, and learning how to pick greens. And she didn't play the radio. Her daughter, Nettie Brown, lived to be 90. My grandfather was 89 when he passed away. And so yeah, we were blessed with some longevity. I spent so much time with them, like whole summers. I didn't understand (how important it was) until I got older because it was like, "you got to go to your grandma's house." And it was aggravating when I was coming up. Now I'm like, that is the biggest blessing I've ever had, I can ever imagine. I sat at the feet of my elders in their 90s. You know what I mean? They were talking about stuff that was happening in the 1800s and 1900s.

Terri: You talked about sitting at the feet of your elders. You talked about learning how to cook. Tell me what else was so great about growing up in Kennedy Homes.

Carla: Oh gosh. Kennedy Homes was one of those places that everybody was looking out for everybody. I think it was the time, the era that we lived in. Definitely in Kennedy Homes they had some stuff going on out there. You know what I mean? Because, for one, my grandmother was a bootlegger. And she made her own buck. Buck is made from fermented fruit and potatoes. Yessuh! Listen to me good, that was some moonshine, that would have you so drunk. People would come and get it.

She would have it in these milk jugs. And she would tell my uncles all the time, "Hey, go breathe my jugs." And so, one of my uncles, the lazy one, I won't call his name, but he'll tell her, "I already breathed it." If you didn't do that the bottles would swell. He didn't do it. And so, one day, she's in there, and there's this exploding sound; everything's everywhere.

My grandmothers were pistol packing and knife-toting, you know, stand up for themselves kind of women. My great-grandmother lived on one side of Kennedy Homes. and my grandmother lived on the other side in the same section. And it was funny because prior to them moving there, there were no outside flowers. Everybody knew my people because she always had her own garden, her own flowers.

I remember one of my fondest stories, and one of the funniest things I've ever seen is my great-grandmother who was not the bootleg lady, but the root lady. It was so funny. The boys used to like to play around her garden, and they would throw the football and have to run through her plants. And she kept telling them to stop. One of the kids mouthed off to her, and she said, "Okay." She was crippled from an automobile accident. And when he said something to her, to make fun of her disability. Oh boy! She said, "While you making fun of me make sure you don't break your leg while you're out there playing." And he broke his leg while he was out there playing. And from that day on, nobody ever played in front of our door - kids were not allowed to come around there.

They knew my mom - and my daddy was very popular - one because he was the weed man. But also because he was "that guy" in the 70s. And so, he was flashy and all the things that the weed man was, you know, he had the big sports car. He had a Nova that was hot, hiked up in the back. An Impala for my mama. And, you know, they had all of the things. And so, we were very, very popular in Kennedy Homes for a lot of reasons.

Terri: Did you still have family there when they mercilessly closed Kennedy Homes down with the promise that they were going to rebuild and bring y'all back?

Carla: I could say I had some family there because my uncle had married a lady there. That was my aunt, you know, and she got displaced. I was there for a large portion of that entire transition. I was there for the grand movement that they made into the University Center Hotel. You remember that? I was also there when the University Center Hotel had to close, shut down.

I remember passing by there one day, and it wasn't me feeling sorry for the hotel - but somebody had their bicycles on the balcony, and they were kind of hanging over. And somebody had made a clothesline in the back. And that's when I realized the magnitude of what had happened. Y'all just made all these people homeless. Being inside of that hotel did not give them a home. That place fell apart around them folks.

It's a shame. I remember one of the persons, I think it was Vanessa, who was trying to do some of the advocacy around the Kennedy Homes and trying to get us this little bit of a stipend, like the ones from the former president. And I was like, listen, we're in a crisis. This is not no money!

Nobody gave us a gift! And when you look at the crisis that we're in (COVID) versus what they put in our hand! That's the way I look at Kennedy Homes. The same way. The crisis that they were in versus that little bit of a couple of pennies that they got was a shame. And every single solitary person was displaced. Every last one of them.

I remember that. Yeah. I remember helping out a couple of people while they were there, and I went and looked inside - and the hotel that they put them in didn't really leave room for activity. It was more secluded.

And you know, they didn't think about the best option. What will we do with the children? They didn't think about any of that. No. They just stuffed them somewhere so that the media could stop (talking).

And so, yeah, I remember. Thankfully, my grandmother had just received her housing. She moved into a house away from Kennedy Homes, like months prior to that. She and my mom's youngest sister. They both got houses through the Gainesville Housing Authority, Section 8 Program. And a little while later, there was no more Kennedy Homes.

Terri: And so back to your story. Kennedy Homes and Seminary Lane are problem spots for Gainesville history. But I really would love to see the city acknowledge their folly and really go ahead and define what affordable housing is so we can introduce it back into our society. And I don't think it will ever, it will not happen in my lifetime.

Carla: I stay away from "affordable housing" because housing is not affordable. Affordable housing is relative to how much income you make. How cheap you build it and make it; it can be $25,000. If people are still redlining, if they're still doing predatory loans, if they're still discriminating at the bank, "Who gonna give me $25,000 to get it?" I don't care how much it costs.

And then when you are inside of a home and you look at the cost of a home, you know what I'm saying? Like, I'm gonna take my daughter as a prime example. She had a fire in her kitchen. A couple of days off from work, she had two days off from work, right? So now what my check gonna look like? And then her car broke down. Now, all of a sudden, she's three weeks behind on everything.

Without my parents and me coming to say, "Hey, collective economics and building family and holding each other up." Without that, we all one check away (from being in the same position). One check. You know, I experienced the same thing you know. It doesn't matter how much you make, even over $75,000. And that's why I say people used to think about, you know, $15 an hour - as a living wage? You can pay people $30, $40 an hour, and they won't be able to live. You know what I mean? A prime example. I've been trying to tuck away and every time I seem like I get a little savings, here comes something. And then it's back to paycheck to paycheck. You know, you're stuck in that cycle.

Someone said about the work that I do, "You've been doing this for Duval for how long?" I said I believe in the Community Development Corporation, but I can't lift that off the ground and lift this organization, that's UF - and right now, they got the money to pay me. She was like, "Oh, I didn't know it was about money for you." I said, help me understand why the United Way executive director, I mean, chief executive officer, makes two hundred and twelve thousand dollars a year. The executive director makes one hundred and sixty-five thousand dollars a year. Nobody questions them about anything - yet, here I am slaving like a dog, taking my personal money to have programming and stuff for my seniors. And as soon as I say I want a salary, they tell me that it's a damn shame.

That is how I got involved with one of the young men that's now working for SPARC, and I understand his mom's concept. But for me, you know me, I'm always looking at solutions. And so, I saw this guy, this baby who had this beautiful drawing, beautiful talent. And I said to his mom, "I want him in my summer program and want him to do something. What is he doing this summer?"

She said, "He need to find him a real job because that drawing ain't going to cut it." But here this kid is creating a masterpiece, a self-portrait of folk in less than an hour and 15 minutes. And what she's saying is he hasn't been able to get paid for this. For me, it's not about finding him a job at Burger King to make up the difference. It's about creating opportunities for him to work and do his art. I told her, "You know, that's one of the things I want us to stop doing. Saying that artists need to get a "real job" because that's a real job. You know, what we need to do is make sure they have an opportunity; where if I'm a videographer, I don't have to moonlight at the insurance company."

But it's another testament to our city, we're always looking on the outside for talent and looking on the outside instead of trying to develop and helping local artists with so-called procurement processes that empower our own community. Because there's enough work. We're just not the ones that's getting it.

Terri: Tell me about what you do in Duval.

Carla: Duval is where I've been since I was three. I was raised in that community. And also, in the area that they call Lake Road. People look at Duval and assume that we were growing. We had divisions in the individual community.

Habitat for Humanity (HFH) came in to do some, they said neighborhood revitalization. HFH created a paint program where they were going to paint some houses, and they were going to do some critical home repairs, like roofs. And I was like, "How does that revive the neighborhood? That's not what revitalization is. That's like putting paint over some mold."

The mold is still gonna grow through the paint. Why would you come through the neighborhood and paint a house that is failing, that is many thousands of dollars behind on taxes. Why would you come in and paint that house? Why don't you help the person inside the house? If y'all got money, 'cause they had some funds, that was a big thing. They had resources. If y'all got some resources, let's do revitalization another way.

And that is how my mom was like, "Well, get some neighbors together and tell us what we should be doing." And so, my mom started this organization and scheduled this big meeting with HFH to come out and they were really excited because it was the most residents they had seen. And we were talking about forming this organization and I would just come for the barbecue. I don't say no to some good barbecue.

They had just finished a project in our neighborhood where the city had seven hundred or something thousand dollars. And they asked the community to come together to decide on a project and we wouldn't go. But then they unveiled their big flowerpot that sits at the intersection of East University and Hawthorne Road. They had some Black community leaders, older women, who thought that that was the most fabulous thing. They showed up to the meetings. They designed it. They had so many palm trees that they were giving away twenty thousand dollar trees down there, and we got people's houses falling in. So much vacancy.

After that, I started going to meetings. But I still don't have no faith in the process right? I went to that meeting with my mom. Like I said, they had some David's barbecue there and they were making a point about neighborhood revitalization and how they would go about it. And I raised my hand and whatever I said, the people started clapping and they stood up. I finished eating my barbecue.

Afterward, here comes a reporter. Reporting on this thing that Habitat was doing. Wanted to talk to that resident that made that point and that was the center of the thing. And I talked to her. And things just started to grow. My mom called us to a meeting at Dayspring Church. She and Annette Burkett, who was the other person that was working with her to get all these residents together. And we're going to start this organization, and we need some temporary folks to come in. And I'm sitting there and she's like, "And my daughter is going to..." So, I was "voluntold."

And then she was like, "She's going to be the president."

And me not understanding anything about organizations, I was like, "I don't want to be the president and do all that work. I'll do something else. What's up under the president? Vice president?"

"Hmmm, somebody else wanted that position."

And I was like, "Yeah."

And she was like, "Well, secretary?"

I was like, "Yeah, I can answer the phone and type." We started the Greater Duval Neighborhood Association.

In the midst of that I started a group called Diamonds in the Rough. And this is when everything about advocacy for me changed. I started working with Habitat, and I was going to do this home ownership thing for them, and I was going to get girls from Gardenia (subsidized apartments in the Duval community), and I wanted to put them into housing. We had this pipeline, and we were going to do all this great work. And then I started working on that with them one by one, and I realized that, these are some of the women that I used to get high with." And they are still in the middle of their addiction. So, it became more like case management.

And then I said, "You know what? I'm going to create a program just for the kids of addicts." because I started recognizing too some of the faces I saw were actually the little kids who mamas I used to sit in the bedroom with, maybe in the living room. I felt an obligation to them.

I started working with them and started kids' programs and programs for seniors and started Diamonds in the Rough. And I got my first person. I'm going to move her to home ownership. I found out she could not read. So, no, she didn't have a job. We're going to get her job. She didn't have a high school diploma. We're going to get her a high school diploma. She couldn't read. I'm going to help her read. She's dealing with trauma. She's been raped. She's been molested. And now is the problem (really) - affordable housing?

I was like, "Okay, Lord, I need to go regroup." And we started and kept on with the summer program and just made it focus on youth empowerment. We take high risk kids, kids that are in trouble and expose them to all types of careers. Careers that they actually get to experience. And so that's why we call it Summer Sling, because we're just chunking stuff at them, and seeing what sticks.

We do arts and culture, but we also have a component that deals with trauma, with conflict resolution, with dealing with feelings, and letting them know that they have a support system.
We were going to do two years with kids, and we were going to be done. I have kids that are graduating, that still keep in contact with me. We follow them through high school. We have been their tutors. My partner, Andrew Miles has been to the schools for parents that don't know how to navigate that.

That is not what our organization is supposed to be doing. But every year we do something new. I added that to the by-laws. And yeah, this is what we exist for, because it's just – the needs are so great. That was the start of the Greater Duval Neighborhood Association. But my first activist project was the Clarence R. Kelly Center.

I knew Clarence R. Kelly, Mr. Kelly, who was my camp counselor, was also the counselor for my kids once they were of age to go. He had a massive heart attack and died - out the blue. And it was my understanding that there was some provision made, or his family was saying that he wanted to give so much for our people, to the city. NOT! You should never have given anything - that should've gone to your family. But he had a desire to feed into the life of children. But the city came and decided that they were going to shut down the Clarence R. Kelly Center after they built the Martin Luther King Center (MLK). And that all of the kids could go across that busy Waldo Road Highway to get to the MLK. And that's when my activism started. The first thing we advocated for was to reopen the center. My next activism was for them to actually put money and resources into it. My organization started partnering with them on gardening and science projects, programs in partnership with Cultural Arts Coalition and Ms. Nkwanda Jah. We brought some science programs there. We brought gardening programs there. We had our own after school and tutoring. And there were like 45 students there, but the center started failing. And they came up with that 'Wild Spaces, Public Places' thing. And they came to us and was like, "Hey, you know we're trying to get a tax that'll help fix stuff like the Clarence R. Kelly Center. You should really come and work on our campaign."

Because one of the first things we'll do is remodel this center, I mean, for the community. We got to get the Black folks. We got to get them to buy in, Carla. And there I go with my boots on, knocking on doors and making the calls, for the tax and yay, we got it!

And the first thing they did was go make upgrades to the golf course. They started looking at projects all around, all this new stuff. Thank God for our allies because I had a person come to me and say, "They can really take Clarence R. Kelly off the project list." I said, "What project list?" He said, "Oh, there were 99 projects that were supposed to be built that was a part of the campaign. This is what they said to get the money." And so, I wanted to know what else was being taken off of that list. And he gave me the list.

A couple of weeks go by, and this same person come to me and say, "There's an opening on the Wild Spaces, Public Places board, that way you can get all this information firsthand." And I said, "Thank you." And they were really surprised to see me show up in that space. Needless to say, a little while later, the Clarence R. Kelly Center went back on that list along with Unity Park and some other parks that they were going to wait until the next round of funding came through, whatever that was.

And then right before COVID, they were like, "Let's remodel it." Right? A Black contractor, One Day, came; and they had a plan to hire 90% of their people from the community to work with the guys that used to hang out outside the store and do all this wonderful work, and then COVID hit. And then Lee Feldman came. He sent it back out to bid, and One Day could not compete for the bid. And we lost it to another contractor who did agree to work with us on the design. We did a series of community meetings where we put our input in the design, and they built us a center. It is two years old and has had 25 leaks in it. They need to replace the whole $45,000 roof and also need a new air conditioning system.

Terri: Representing Kennedy Holmes and Duval. Thank you for all your hard work. Before I let you go, you know another part of my project is talking about Black music in Gainesville as experienced by Black folks. And you told me about a very unique story. Please share it.

Carla: That same bootlegging great grandma that I talked about, in her early life was also what you call a barmaid. She would travel the Chitlin Circuit with all types of musicians. And she traveled with them. First, let me tell you the story of how I got my head almost knocked off my shoulders. I also used to travel with reggae artists anywhere they went. I liked traveling with reggae artists because (before the world got crazy) they would never separate themselves from their fans. They perform, they leave the stage, they go sit down and have a drink. It was easy to meet anybody you wanted to meet. All you had to do was go to the concert. They're coming to town and you're going to see them. You had celebrities coming to town asking about this Mom's Kitchen place, or Momma Lo's, and then they wanted to know where the weed was.

I told my grandmother because I, at the time, classified myself and was classified by others as a groupie. So, I told my grandmother, and she was like, "Well, you know I travel with blues singers on the Chitlin' Circuit."

And I said, "Oh you was a groupie." She said, "No ma'am. I was not a groupie. What you doing is groupie. You spending your money. I was making money."

She told me that was different. But what she would do, because Black people were not allowed in these restaurants, was find people in different towns, and they would get together and she would be the one to make sure that their clothes were clean, ironed, and that they had everything they needed. She ran their errands. She was the one going to the stores and the back doors trying to get them the things that they needed. But she was a part of the group.

But more importantly than that, growing up, I remember one, two o'clock in the morning, being alarmed awake by a blast of loud music. And I would get to the hallway, get down low and I would see people, musicians, and people dancing. My great grandmother, even though she was paralyzed, she'd get up on her walker - baby she'd be doing her thing.

They were in there dancing and doing all of their things. My daddy loved music. My grandfather was complete nuts over music. That's where I got my love for reggae music from and my love for dancing, from my dad. Whenever the grown folk came, it was always that one kid that called on and I was that kid.

"Carla, come out here and do a li'l something!" They'd be good and drunk. Now my great grandmother had a good ring in her and she drank for fun. My grandmother was an alcoholic. And her drinking always led to her waking up all the kids. And then, if you didn't wake up, she's going to pinch you 'til you did. And here we are in the living room with these grown ass men, and she'd want us to dance. We in our pajamas, we tired or whatever. But I would recognize these faces and see these people.

When I was about 16, 17, because you know we don't have internet, I'm looking at something on TV and I'm just casually commenting to my mom that B.B. King was coming to Lowell Prison and he was going to perform because his daughter was in prison and had been telling her jail mates, "Hey, this is my daddy." And of course nobody believed her. I told my mom, "You know who B.B. King always reminds me. The one used to come through playing music and stuff and we would get woken up when he was at the house. He reminds me of him." And she said, "That's because it's the same person."

She showed me pictures of people like Muddy Waters, and somebody named Howlin' Wolf and all these people. She was like, "You remember him? You remember him? You remember him?" And I was like, "What in the world?" They would pass through her place because one, she was familiar and they trusted her and they knew she would have everything that they wanted, but they would be going back or leaving places like St. Augustine, Tampa, different places, and then heading back up north. They would come through Gainesville.

And I'm looking at these pictures that my mom has and I'm like, "So, two o'clock in the morning in Kennedy Holmes' apartments, you're trying to tell me that B.B. King was sitting in my grandma's living room, and I was dancing in the middle of the floor while he was there." That's what she was trying to tell me. And she was like, "Yes." And then she reminded me of the same daughter that he was coming to perform for. "You remember the little girl that we kept for a little while? And her momma's name is so-and-so?" And I said, "Oh, yeah, because we went to high school together." And she still remembers us from being young. And then she started telling us, "Yeah, I used to date Ray Charles, too." Now, mind you, at the time, Ray Charles was a lot larger than life.

And a lot more successful in a lot of ways than a lot of the other people who she had showed us, right? And so, we had started hearing about all these stories about her and Ray Charles and Ray Charles this and Ray Charles that. She talked about one of the things that she remembered is that he would always, touch a woman's wrist - and mind you, no movie had come out. She died in 93. But we got the whole story. When she was sick, we found out Ray Charles was coming to the Center for Performing Arts. The couple that was working with her knew someone at the center.

And asked, "Can you reach his public relations people for us? We have a client, a patient that says she's a friend of his, and we want to know, does he remember her?"

She agreed to do it. We gave her the details and was like – whatever. She called back and asked, "Is her name Ethel May? "Oh yeah, he knows her." And they were able to get them together. She sat in the C-section, had her on the front row, took her backstage, met with her, talked with her. They laughed and brought back memories like two old friends. And she was like, "You know what? I'm going to start me a scrapbook and I'm fin' to reach out to all my buddies." Because she was like, "We dated, but for the most part, they were just my friends." The Scene Magazine at the time did an article about him coming to town, but the Gainesville Sun did an article about him and her titled "Charles Meets an Old Flames." She held on to those tickets until death.

GAINESVILLE PROPER

ON HER MIND

Charles meets an old flame

By ANDREA BILLUPS
Sun correspondent

Ethel Graham said her prayers. Restless and unable to sleep, she recited the 23rd Psalm and then said her prayers again.

But even divine guidance could not contain her excitement and bring her slumber.

Confined to a wheelchair and unable to get out much, she had just returned from the Center for Performing Arts and a surprise meeting with a man she dated decades ago, the musical legend and star of the show, Ray Charles.

"It brought back so many memories," Graham said Sunday.

"He looked marvelous," she said. "He's the same, himself, outgoing and kind. He still has that good sense of humor. He hasn't changed."

More than 40 years ago, Graham worked as a barmaid at the Little Savoy, a hotel and lounge on Central and Scott in west Tampa.

Featured on the bill was a young, blind piano player, unknown, but beginning to make his mark with a bluesy style that was hard to forget. Graham brought him drinks.
See MEET on page 6A

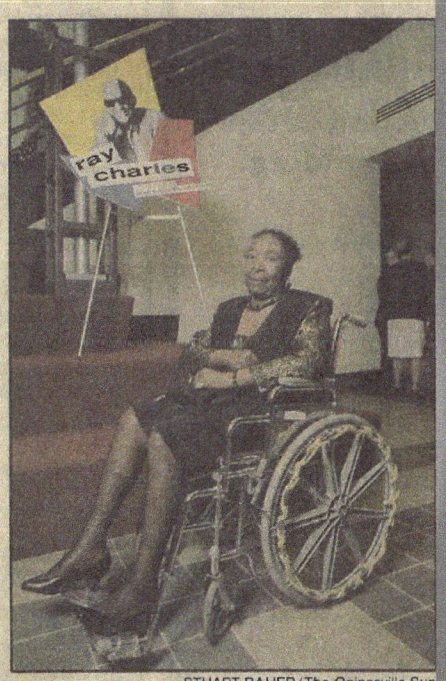

STUART BAUER/The Gainesville Sun
Ethel Graham was reunited with a man she dated in Tampa, Ray Charles, after his concert Saturday night at the Center for the Performing Arts.

MEET

Continued from page 1A

He was funny and always making jokes, she remembers. And he was a perfectionist, rehearsing songs over and over until he got things just right.

"One thing led to another," Graham said, and the two struck up a friendship.

Charles and a five-piece band made the rounds of local clubs and Graham and her girlfriends would carpool around to see all his gigs. This continued for a year or so, until Charles took his act north, where there was more money to be made.

Charles

The rest, as they say, is show biz history.

Ray Charles became a star, a musical genius. Billy Joel named his daughter Alexa Ray after him. At 61, he's still in demand, seen playing "Georgia on My Mind," for the opening credits of CBS's "Designing Women" and proclaiming, "You Got the Right One, Baby," in a memorable Diet Pepsi TV commercial.

For Graham, now 67, life was more mainstream. She moved from Tampa to Ocala and went on with her life. She got married, raised three daughters and some grandsons.

But she never forgot Charles and his talent. She followed his career, "his ups and his downs," reading everything she could, staying up to see him on television.

Several years ago, while living in Ocala, Graham's life took a downturn. She was in an accident and had spinal surgery that left her incapacitated. She sold her home and moved to Gainesville and has lived here ever since.

She lives alone now but has help getting around. She can stand and walk with assistance. But her injury took its toll on her mentally.

"I'd been fighting this battle for a long time and I had almost given up hope," she said. "I was a very independent person and it was hard needing someone to help me."

Just when she felt like she couldn't carry on, Graham says, she met physical therapist Sara Meeks and her husband, John Harrison. As a part of Graham's treatment, Meeks was assigned to visit Graham's home and work on her rehabilitation. Meek's husband, a massage therapist, joined in her therapy, and the three soon became good friends.

One day, Graham told them about her relationship with Charles. And when Harrison and Meeks heard that Charles was coming to town, they set out to make a dream come true.

They contacted Phyllis Bleiweiss with the Florida Arts Celebration. She wrote the Ray Charles organization and asked if he might remember Graham. He did and, unbeknownst to Graham, a backstage meeting was arranged.

Saturday night Graham's three daughters, Eartha Bing, Joyce Ann Law and Betty Bugg, came to her house to help her do her hair and makeup. They joined together to buy her a new black-and-gold dress.

Inside the center, before the concert, Graham was beaming and was visibly nervous.

"I'm just about ready to pass out," she said. "I've been on cloud nine ever since these beautiful people brought me here."

When the show was over, LeAnn Flynn, the center's marketing director, came to get the group and escorted Graham to Charles' dressing room.

"I though my heart was going to stop," Graham said when they revealed their secret and told her she would meet Charles. "I felt like maybe I could have stood up out of this chair."

Backstage, Graham and Charles exchanged "glad to see yous," and "how have you been's," Graham said.

He took her hands in his and they reminisced about places they had been.

Back home, safely tucked into her bed, but too excited to sleep, Graham says she felt a little reborn herself.

"Everyone was so good to me," she said. "I'll always love and remember them for giving me such a wonderful evening. It's like a new breath of life to get to see him. I'll remember it for the rest of my life."

Pastor Ernestine Brockington Butler: A Healer of the Body, Soul, and Community

I am Pastor Ernestine Brockington Butler. My mother is Addie Brockington. I'll probably talk more about her than my father, Eli, because she was always there.

Of course, she was a Davis,, Addie Davis Brockington. Her parents were Addie and Fernando Davis.

So anyway, coming on down, my mother married into the Brockington family. She tells us that when she married into that family, there were about 17 boys. So, therefore, if you hear the name, Brockington, we're probably all related.

At that time, she said, it was a migration. A lot of them had already gone north. That's where all the big factories and everything was. So, she married into the Brockington family.

One thing that she always told us was that when her mother-in-law's feet hit the floor, she was already dressed and ready to hit the floor, too. Back in the day, when you got married, a lot of times you went and lived in the house with your in-laws.

My mother was more instrumental in our lives because she was always there. Even now, we always say, "what Addie said", or "what Mama said", or "or what Madea said"; because she was such a force in our lives.

Even back then, when Blacks didn't own a lot, my mother was smart enough to rent several houses when she came to Gainesville. What year? I can't tell you.

Terri: You said she came to Gainesville. Where was she from?

Pastor Butler: Originally from the Carolinas. In fact, I think she told us North Carolina was where her family was. In fact, I'm sure because I started dating someone named Davis, and she said, "You better make sure he wasn't from Carolina."

She was quite a force. She learned how to make money and taught us how to. I'm from a very large family. It was 12 of us, and I'm kinda in the middle there. We were born and raised right there off of 5th Avenue, on 6th Place. I was born at home. In fact, my birthday is messed up because my birth wasn't registered until a whole year later. And the date was off, and we used to talk about that all the time. I didn't get my birth certificate until I got into nursing school. A lot of other people were born at home too; and like me they weren't registered until a whole year later.

Terri: You say 6th Place. 6th Place on the side of 6th Street where Dr. Banks and those are or across 6th Street?

Pastor Butler: Northwest. If you look at where A. Quinn Jones is, the next street over would have been 6th Place and then 6th Avenue and then 5th Avenue. I lived right next door to the original Mom's Kitchen.

Terri: That is interesting. I wasn't even aware that there was another Mom's Kitchen.

Pastor Butler: Yeah, that was where it was originally. That building looked like a house. It was originally a little shop by Miss Mamie. And when Miss Ada Lu and Mamie gave it up, that's when the Youngs, Mr. Frank and Miss Lula Mae Young purchased it.

Terri: Tell me about growing up on 5th Avenue, Crosstown.

Pastor Butler: It was wonderful. Back in the day, Blacks owned all the businesses and everything up and down 5th Avenue. Yes, sir. One of my favorite places that we could go to when we were young was the Rose Theater. And for a quarter, you could see a matinee movie, usually a cartoon, the whole nine yards. It was quite a treat for us.

But what was a more wonderful treat was going home. We would stop at Reverend Cato's. And for a quarter, I could have a cherry root beer and a hot dog, grilled bun with all the fixings on it.

Again, all of the businesses up and down 5th Avenue were Black-owned and operated. The shoe shop - Mr. Oscar Gilbert was there. The little grocery store was there, and there were several eating places. A lot of people remember Mama Lowe's, but before that, back off 5th Avenue, was Annie McCray's. For a little of nothing, you know, you go there, and you get this big plate of food. And hey, three or four people could literally eat off it.

Terri: Ms. Annie's? Behind Woody's?

Paster Butler: Yes. Yes, ma'am.

Terri: That was Northwest 7th Terrace. And that's where my grandparents lived when I was born. It was Ms. Annie's, and then it was Ms. Mercedes, her mother, and her son Dale, the Williams, and then the daycare center, Bell Nursery. And then Ms. Ollie Mae's house.

Pastor Butler: The whole story back in the day used to be, everyone was related to the Youngs, the Brockingtons, or the Warrens. Because we had the largest families in that area. One of my pastors used to say that all the time if you're from anywhere close to Gainesville, those are the three families that you related to. And back in the day, everything was done community and family-wise.

Before Mr. Frank Young owned Mom's Kitchen, he worked at Humpty Dumpty. That was an eating place right on 13th Street. And back in the day, stuff like the tip of the chicken wing, the gizzards, the liver, and the necks, they didn't sell that. So, on the weekend, he was allowed to fry all that up, and they would bring it into the neighborhood. My brother and his son would go over there and get some, and the cupcakes. And hey, when they came, everybody came out of their houses with their tin plates and their hot sauce. And everybody sat and ate, you know, and that's how it was. You know, back then, if one family had it, everybody had what they needed.

My mother was such an entrepreneur even way back in her time. We were the first ones to have a station wagon. And we used to pile everybody into that station wagon. We had a bunch of friends - and we would go to the drive-in. It would be so many of us stacked in that car. But when we got there, you put your blankets on the ground, and you got the little sound things, and you put them down so everybody got to hear.

My mother's sister, Adela, worked in a place, I don't know if you remember, the little sandwiches and things, used to be in the machines and hospitals and various places like that. Well, that's where she worked. Every couple of days, they had to switch out all those sandwiches. So of course, she would bring them home. We had all our friends come and eat. My brother, Ralph, (who has gone to glory now), he was considered the fastest in the state of Florida.

Terri: Wow! The fastest runner?

Pastor Butler: Fastest runner. Yes ma'am. At Lincoln, his nickname was Road Runner. He was sent to Texas by the J.S. for national track. He swears he won. Back then they didn't have the photo finishes. He ran against Mercury Morris (former Miami Dolphins running back, who died in September 2024). They gave it to Mercury Morris, but my brother Raph swear to God, that he was the winner, and we believed him. So anyway, he would run home and get all the good sandwiches first. I always had pimento cheese.

My sister Barb was also on the track team at Lincoln. She was also a majorette. I was a little, you know, chubby, but I made the pep squad because I couldn't do any splits and jumps. I used to sit in the stand with a whole group of people, and we would help cheer the team on.

We had a very loving family. Our community was little back then, but it was loving and kind. We had a lot of professionals who lived right around us. So, as kids, there were teachers, a mailman. a policeman, a lot of beauticians, we had all those people in our neighborhood. All right there. So, as children, we saw that and respected that.

They were allowed to discipline us. Back in the day, we also had truant officers. So, if you missed school, they knew immediately. And they start riding the neighborhood. But I did learn a few tricks from my brother about how to get out of school. You found some sting nettles, a little plant that if you hit yourself with it, you'll welt up, and they'll send you home. My brothers taught me that.

But anyway, family was extremely important. Churches were extremely important. People went to church. They made sure that their children were in church. Generation to generation. Churches were important. And that's something I think we, as a people, have lost.

Terri: You mentioned multiple neighborhoods. Did you eventually move away from Crosstown and live in one of the other neighborhoods?

Pastor Butler: Yes, I lived in Lincoln Estates. Unfortunately, one of my brothers was killed in a drunk driving type of accident. He and his best friend were only 22 years old. The drunk driver didn't die. He was my namesake, Ernest. With some of the money my mother got from the accident, we moved to Lincoln Estates. We were so proud to have a brand new house out in Lincoln Estates. That was up an up-and-coming neighborhood. It was wonderful. Most people don't realize that a lot of the Blacks were not allowed to buy property. And there was this man, who was an attorney that would help Blacks get their places. That was a little before we moved out there.

That neighborhood was family-oriented, too. The people that lived close together, they stuck together. And we would have to walk to Lincoln High School, which started in seventh grade. I remember back then we girls weren't allowed to wear pants. So, on those cold days, you learned to put the pants on under the dress and go on to school.

We lived out there until I was grown and got married and moved over here to Duval

Terri: Does your family still own your home from those days?

Pastor Butler: Oh, yes. Like I said, my mother always taught us to take care of one another, to be there for one another. When my mother passed, my sister got the house because all the rest of us owned our own homes.
.

Terri: And you got married and moved to Duval. How has it been living over here?

Pastor Butler: I moved over here before I was married. Okay. I moved into the house that I'm living in now. And every now and then I get this spirit that I want to move. And then I find out the price of houses, then I calm down. But yes, I moved into the house that I'm in now. And I did get married. But even prior to that, I had a daughter, you know, not listening. And my daughter was born, but I still went on to school.

I would catch the bus to nursing school. As far as I was concerned, I wasn't supposed to be a nurse. I was supposed to be a doctor. I graduated from nursing school at Santa Fe Community College. You know, back in the day, you could go to Santa Fe and take as many classes as you wanted for $75.

I worked for Alachua General. Then Alachua General was acquired by Shands. I was a nurse for 48 years. I still have my nursing license, but in my latter years, I did substance abuse, and I did lectures, and the people I lectured were doctors, lawyers, Indian chiefs, and so forth.

Terri: How long have you been a pastor?

Pastor Butler: I have been a pastor for close to 20 years. I started off, of course, like everybody else, just going to church. And you hear people say they have that calling. You know, mine was teaching, you know, and I was okay with that. And the clients that I had in substance abuse, I talked to them about spiritual issues, which was okay because, you know, God grant me the serenity... We talked a lot about that, and a lot of people I talked to were doctors and lawyers because, at that time, Florida Recovery Center or Shands had the contract for LPN and PRN, which are your professionals. I talked with a lot of them, about forgiving and loving. It doesn't matter if you're a saint, can't, ain't, Buddhist, whatever. Pain is pain; hurt is hurt, depression is depression, and sadness is sadness. I don't care what you are. And so, I talked with a lot of those clients.

One of the people that they had brought to Shands to take over the substance program, called me into his office one day and told me that there was one factor that all the people that he was seeing had in common - me talking about spiritual issues. So, I thought, okay, God, that's my calling.

I sat under the late great Apostle Ron Thomas for 30 plus years. I became one of the elders, I guess 20 plus years I was ordained. But I did not go back to school to get a degree in theology until maybe about close to eight, 10 years ago. But I was already ordained as a pastor.

Terri: Do you currently have a church?

Pastor Butler: Agape Faith Center. I am now the senior pastor there. Ron Thomas was the founding pastor after he, it was his wife, Pastor Marvynell. And she stepped down. I was her assistant for many years, and I became the senior pastor of Agape Faith Center.

Terri: One last thing I would love to ask you about is your senior group here at the Clarence R. Kelley Center.

Pastor Butler: Love it, love it, love it. We are under the umbrella of Greater Duvall Neighborhood Association. We call ourselves "Seniors on the Move". I'm the president of this group. You name it, we try to do it. We bring in a lot of various groups, organizations, things that will benefit the Black community. Case in point, we had voter registration. We actually had Kim Barton, the Supervisor of Elections send a whole team down here and we got registered.

I try to always bring people to my group. Yes. We've had Community Redevelopment Agency come. We've gotten free air conditioning from the City. We've had house painting done. We've had our property taxes lowered. My thing is to bring something to the table that's going to benefit my ladies and gents. But one of the things that we love more than anything, or they love more than anything, is Bingo Thursday.

They get, I mean, whatever. But we have been doing this for many years. We love it. We've had other communities come in to copy us because we are a 501c3 and we are organized. We have been around for about 10 years, and a lot of organizations, as you know, start and stop. But we have been here. We've been a staple. Not only that, but I also team up with Bread of the Mighty Food Pantry through Agape Faith Center, and I make sure some days that they leave with a bag of something nutritious.

Terri: Please tell us a little bit about the Quilt Project.

Pastor Butler: Oh wow. We got some grant money for the Quitting Project. Not only us, but numerous organizations. So, we started making a memory quilt. First, it was just around grief. But then we said, "Let's make it memories." You know, so it's a memory quilt that we will have a presentation of. Only one or two of us were actually seamstresses who knew how to sew. And so, the rest of us, we've been sewing flying by the seat of our pants. But we've done a great job. So, we brought in pictures of loved ones or whatever you want. Some put flowers there. There are numerous things. And then we put it all together and made a quilt.

GAINESVILLE PROPER

GAINESVILLE PROPER

TERRI L. BAILEY, MA

Alachua County

There is so much more to Alachua County
Than our Gator claim to fame
Nature offerings like Paynes Prairie
Make people remember our name

Gainesville was once known as tree city
And also, for that Gainesville Green
Though developers are trying to concrete us up
Lush landscapes still pepper the scene

Micanopy and Waldo recall the past
With a host of antique boutiques
Alachua is growing fast
With many unique eateries deemed country chic

The name High Springs is appropriate
For there are Cool Waters galore
They have camping grounds, caves, and nature trails
Offering family fun and more

Hawthorne trail provides scenic routes
That give bikers a breathtaking view
And Archer welcomed Rosewood families
Who had to flee from racist terror and start up life anew

LaCrosse is quite famous for its farming
And its innovative crops
Newberry's host of old architecture
Made it a necessary historical stop

Alachua County is trying to develop
A cultural arts legacy
With sculpture, dance, poetry and murals
Adding aesthetics to the heart of our cities

Our county's past ain't all sunshine and roses
We do have some dark history
Though it's etched in our mind
Through darkness we'll shine
As we create a rich new legacy

A Call to Action

There is a growing concern that the areas across Waldo Road are rapidly following the path of Crosstown and Porters Quarters. The resources in several historically Black neighborhoods are noticeably depleted. However, the neighborhood associations in these targeted areas are not backing down. They are assertively holding elected officials and government agencies accountable, demanding that they fulfill their promises to preserve the history and culture of our remaining historically Black communities.

One powerful way to combat gentrification is for families to take responsibility for passing on generational wealth through land ownership and estate planning. The original family landowners of these properties must take action, creating irrevocable trusts, designating heirs, and leaving clear-cut instructions for family properties. It's crucial to make a list of potential heirs in case the designated one passes away. Engage in open and honest conversations with your children and their children about the hard work and sacrifices that Big Momma and Granddaddy made to acquire this property. Share stories of triumph and tragedy to help them understand the direct connection between their blood and the land. Present this task as a noble duty, explaining that those entrusted with this responsibility will ensure that the family legacy and name are preserved for future generations.

Imagine the potential if we pooled our community's financial resources and sought wealthy partners who share our vision of affordable housing for all. This collective action could create more stable and sustainable communities rather than just more profits. When properties in the neighborhood become available, the community could purchase them and create the affordable housing that we so desperately need. This is a powerful strategy that can bring families and neighbors back to our streets, giving us hope for a brighter future.

Acknowledgements

This book was made possible by a grant from SPARC352, The Mellon Foundation, The University of Florida College of the Arts, and the Center for Arts and Medicine and the Center for Arts, Migration + Entrepreneurship. My most sincere appreciation for choosing my project.

Thanks to the Bailey Learning and Arts Collective, Inc. for their fiscal sponsorship and use of the space at the Santa Fe College Center of Innovation and Economic Development.

Much love and appreciation to my hubby, Turbado Marabou, daughter Aaliyah (and her caregivers Glori, Christina, and Chalyn, Nae) and family for putting up with me constantly discussing, stressing, and lamenting over this project at all hours of the day and night.

A heartfelt thank you to Lorenza Lo Weaver and DWMT Productions for all the videos, impromptu interviews, stills, and transcripts and to E. Claudette Freeman of Pecan Tree Publishing for all the edits, advice and extended patience with this first-time author.

Thanks to Nat Tucci, for all the transcribing work she did, simply for the love of hearing the stories.

Special shout out to my interns Danelle D'Angelo and Malachi Dixon for help with grant writing and transcription.

Thanks to all the folks who took the time to share stories, photos, and feelings about gentrification. (My apologies to Mrs. Esther Thomas for the accidental deletion of your story. Your story, photos, and memories will be in volume two.)

1. Alexandria Gibson
2. Carlos Nelson
3. Carolyn Edwards
4. Connie Rawls
5. Darryl King Porters
6. Delvon Filer
7. Domonique Pinder
8. Gerard Duncan
9. Henry Leath
10. Janice and Jimmy Ellis
11. Marriette Ellis
12. Alyne Harris
13. Mary Perry Issac
14. Carla Lewis
15. Ms. Patricia J Powers
16. Ernestine Butler
17. Peter King
18. Robert Jammer
19. Rosa B. Williams
20. Sam Wesley
21. Sharnda Mosley
22. Tabatha Williams
23. Tanisha Byers
24. Tina Certain
25. Tonia Potter
26. Turbado Marabou
27. Vivian Filer Interview
28. Yvette Clark

References

Black Heritage North Central Florida. (n.d.). Alachua County/Gainesville. In *Black Heritage North Central Florida: Alachua, Columbia, Gadsden, Hamilton, and Taylor Countiews* (pp. 1–16). essay.

Beltran, N. (2024). Revisiting porters quarters: the ongoing challenge with gentrification. The Independent Alligator.

Merriam-Webster. (n.d.). Gentrification. In Merriam-Webster.com dictionary. Retrieved August 26, 2024, from https://www.merriam-webster.com/dictionary/gentrification

Thomas, V. (2024, March 15). *Gainesville Housing Authority to update residents on Status of HUD grant*. Gainesville Sun. https://www.gainesville.com/story/news/local/2024/03/15/residents-of-gainesville-housing-authority-to-be-informed-about-hud-grant/72971264007/

Gainesville Neighborhood Voices. (n.d.). https://www.gainesvilleneighborhoodsunited.org/

Photo Credits

Bailey, Terri, 3 2 6 0 1 by Pamela Y. Williams, 28 Aug. 2024. Author's personal collection.
Bailey, Terri, 5th Avenue Business Strip. 25 Sept. 2021. Author's personal collection.
Bailey, Terri, 5th Avenue Construction. 31 Aug. 2022. Author's personal collection.
Bailey, Terri, 5th Avenue Water Tower. 25 Aug. 2024. Author's personal collection.
Bailey, Terri, Airbnb vs Prayers by Faith. 26 Aug. 2024. Author's personal collection.
Bailey, Terri, Barber Shop. 30 Jan. 2021. Author's personal collection.
Bailey, Terri, Boylan School Description. 8 Jun. 2012. Author's personal collection.
Bailey, Terri, Boylan School Jacksonville FL. 8 Jun. 2012. Author's personal collection.
Bailey, Terri, Calvin, and Esther Thomas. 23 Oct. 2024. Author's personal collection.
Bailey, Terri, Charles S. Chestnut Sr. 25 Oct. 2024. Author's personal collection.
Bailey, Terri, Chestnut Funeral Home with Plaque. 27 Sept. 2024. Author's personal collection.
Bailey, Terri, Cosby House. 18 Oct. 2024. Author's personal collection.
Bailey, Terri, Cotton Club Dunbar Hotel. Black Heritage North Central Florida.
Bailey, Terri, Cross Town New Build. 13 Sept. 2024. Author's personal collection.
Bailey, Terri, Dunbar Hotel. Black Heritage North Central Florida.
Bailey, Terri, Duncan Brother's Funeral Home Building. 25 Sept. 2021. Author's personal collection.
Bailey, Terri, Duncan Brother's Funeral Home Entrance. 25 Sept. 2021. Author's personal collection.
Bailey, Terri, Duncan Building. 25 Sept. 2021. Author's personal collection.
Bailey, Terri, Excelsior Matrons with Ma Mese. 25 Oct. 2024. Author's personal collection.
Bailey, Terri, Gainesville Police Department Sign. 9 Aug. 2024. Author's personal collection.
Bailey, Terri, Gentrified Porters Mural. 25 Oct. 2024. Author's personal collection.
Bailey, Terri, Glover, and Gill Building (Wabash Building). 25 Sept. 2021. Author's personal collection.
Bailey, Terri, Hedley House Pleasant Street. 26 Aug. 2024. Author's personal collection..
Bailey, Terri, Henry Leath. 13 Sept. 2024. Author's personal collection.
Bailey, Terri, Josiah T Walls, 25 Oct. 2024. Author's personal collection.
Bailey, Terri, Josiah T. Walls Plague. 13 Sept. 2024. Author's personal collection.
Bailey, Terri, Julia Harper at P.K. Yonge, 25 Oct. 2024. Author's personal collection.
Bailey, Terri, Mount Pleasant United Methodist Church Plaque. 25 Aug. 2024. Author's personal collection.
Bailey, Terri, Mt. Camel Baptist Church Pastors. 22 Sept. 2013. Author's personal collection.

Bailey, Terri, Neighborhood Banners. 13 Sept 2024. Author's personal collection.
Bailey, Terri, New Progressive Church. 25 Sept. 2021. Author's personal collection.
Bailey, Terri, Old Heard House Next to the Water Tower on 5th Avenue. 25 Aug. 2024. Author's personal collection.
Bailey, Terri, Panel 1 SFCC Mural. 12 Apr. 2020. Author's personal collection.
Bailey, Terri, Patricia Powers. 17 Sept. 2024. Author's personal collection.
Bailey, Terri, Pleasant Street Historic District Sign. 25 Aug. 2024. Author's personal collection.
Bailey, Terri, Pleasant Street Historic Society. 5 May 2023. Author's personal collection.
Bailey, Terri, Professor Washington Filer of the Cotton Club Museum and Cultural Center. 12 Aug. 2024. Author's personal collection.
Bailey, Terri, Progressive Church. 25 Sept. 2021. Author's personal collection.
Bailey, Terri, Rev Thomas's House 2024 Renovation. 18 Oct. 2024. Author's personal collection.
Bailey, Terri, Rosa B Williams Art Space. 25 Aug. 2024. Author's personal collection.
Bailey, Terri, Safety Cab Stand. 25 Sept. 2021. Author's personal collection.
Bailey, Terri, Sara McKnight's Pleasant Street Poster. 13 Sept. 2024. Author's personal collection.
Bailey, Terri, Sara McKnight Daughter, and Descendants. 8 Sept. 2024. Author's personal collection.
Bailey, Terri, Terri Bailey and Ms. Karen, 13 Sept. 2024. Author's personal collection.
Bailey, Terri, White & Jones Center. 25 Sept. 2021. Author's personal collection.
Bailey, Terri, Yvonne Ferguson's Sara McKnight Cotton Club Mural. 31 Aug. 2024. Author's personal collection.
Rawls, Connie, Clara's Sign. Rawl's personal collection.
Rawls, Connie, Homecoming 5th Avenue. Rawl's personal collection.
Rawls, Connie, Miss Clara Griffen and her mother Miss Clara. Rawl's personal collection.
Dedicatory Souvenir Program, Old Mount Carmel Baptist Church in 1943. 8 Apr. 1984. George A. Smathers Libraries, University of Florida, Gainesville, Florida.
Duncan, Jackie, McGlon Family. 25 Oct. 2024. Duncan's personal collection.
Edwards, Carolyn, Copy of Dr. Edwards Parent's Wedding Pics. Edwards's personal collection. Taken by Lorenza Edwards.
Edwards, Carolyn, Copy of Dr. Edwards Still. Edwards's personal collection. Taken by Lorenza Edwards.
Edwards, Carolyn, Copy of Dr. Edwards Still Lo Weaver. Edwards's personal collection. Taken by Lorenza Edwards.
Edwards, Carolyn, Copy of Dr. Edwards Still Mom and Grandad, Julius A. Parker. Edward's personal collection. Taken by Lorenza Edwards.
Edwards, Carolyn, Dr. Edwards's Children, Kwesi and Nia, Young Carolyn Lo Weaver Photo. Edward's personal collection. Taken by Lorenza Edwards.
Gibson, Alexandria, Alexandria and B Magic. Gibson's personal collection.
Gibson, Alexandria, Alexandria Gibson and Charlene. Gibson's personal collection.
Harris, Alyne, Spiritual Paintings, Santa Fe Blount Building, Gainesville, Acrylic on Canvas
Jammer, Roberts, Carver Gardens. Jammer's personal collection.
Jammer, Roberts, Robert Jammer. Jammer's personal collection.
Jammer, Roberts, Robert Jammer and Family. Jammer's personal collection.
Jenkins, L. P. R. (2007). *Alachua County Florida*. Arcadia Pub. (Bell Nursey Founder,

Johnson, Maryfran, Redevelopment: City Fights Distrust as It Works to Improve NW 5th Avenue Neighborhood, The Gainesville Sun, 30 Oct. 1978. George A. Smathers Libraries, University of Florida, Gainesville, Florida.

Lincoln High School Protest in Gainesville, Florida. Jan. 1970. George A. Smathers Libraries, University of Florida, Gainesville, Florida.

Lewis, Carla, Carla and her kids. Lewis's personal collection.

Lewis, Carla, Carla's dad. Lewis's personal collection.

Lewis, Carla, Carla on her inch worm. Lewis's personal collection.

Lewis, Carla, Carla's parents. Lewis's personal collection.

Lewis, Carla, Granny. Lewis's personal collection.

Lewis, Carla, Groundbreaking Lewis's personal collection.

Lewis, Carla, Ms. Carla Lewis. Lewis's personal collection.

Marabou, Turbado, Kelly Ctr Mural. 13 Sept. 2024. Marabou's personal collection.

Marabou, Turbado, Heritage Interrupted. Marabou's personal collection.

Porters, Porters Quarter Freedom School Flyer. Porters' personal collection.

Porters, Porters' Paint Party. Porters' personal collection.

Powers, Patricia, Patricia Powers and Dr. Cade. 17 Sept. 2024. Powers's personal collection.

Powers, Patricia, Powers Family. 17 Sept. 2024. Powers's personal collection.

Reverend Willie G. Mayberry, Old Mount Carmel Baptist Church in 1987, George A. Smathers Libraries, University of Florida, Gainesville, Florida.

Sharnda, Susie, Miss Susie Sharnda and Carlos. Sharnda's personal collection.

Sharnda, Susie, Sharnda and Carlos. Sharnda's personal collection.

Thomas, Esther, Ms. Esther Thomas Belk Windows. Thomas's personal collection.

Thomas, Esther, Ms. Esther Thomas. Thomas's personal collection.

The Alachua County Community Remembrance Project, in partnership with J. Micieli-Voutsinas and students from the UF Museum Studies Graduate Program, (2023). "Alachua County Digital Black Heritage Trail Map," UF Research, University of Florida, and the Truth and Reconciliation Commission, Alachua County, FL.

https://truth.alachuacounty.us/files/BHT_Map_Vert_FINAL_B-ADA-Approved.pdf

Williams, Tabitha, Easter Hair. 1 Dec. 2020. William's personal collection.

www.ingramcontent.com/pod-product-compliance
Lightning Source LLC
LaVergne TN
LVHW070530070526
838199LV00075B/6748